THE ODES OF HORACE

THE ODES
OF HORACE

Horatius Flaccus, Quintus

NEWLY TRANSLATED
FROM THE LATIN
AND RENDERED INTO
THE ORIGINAL METRES
BY HELEN ROWE HENZE

UNIVERSITY OF OKLAHOMA PRESS : NORMAN

BY HELEN ROWE HENZE

Song to Life (Boston, 1948)
Each Man's World (Kansas City, Mo., 1950)
Strange Is the Heart (Kansas City, Mo., 1951)
Arise My Love (New York, 1953)
The Odes of Horace (tr.) (Norman, 1961)

THE PUBLICATION OF THIS VOLUME
HAS BEEN AIDED BY A GRANT
FROM THE FORD FOUNDATION.

LIBRARY OF CONGRESS CATALOG CARD NUMBER: 61–15146
Copyright 1961 by the University of Oklahoma Press,
Publishing Division of the University.
Composed and printed at Norman, Oklahoma, U.S.A.,
by the University of Oklahoma Press. First edition.

TO D. HERBERT ABEL

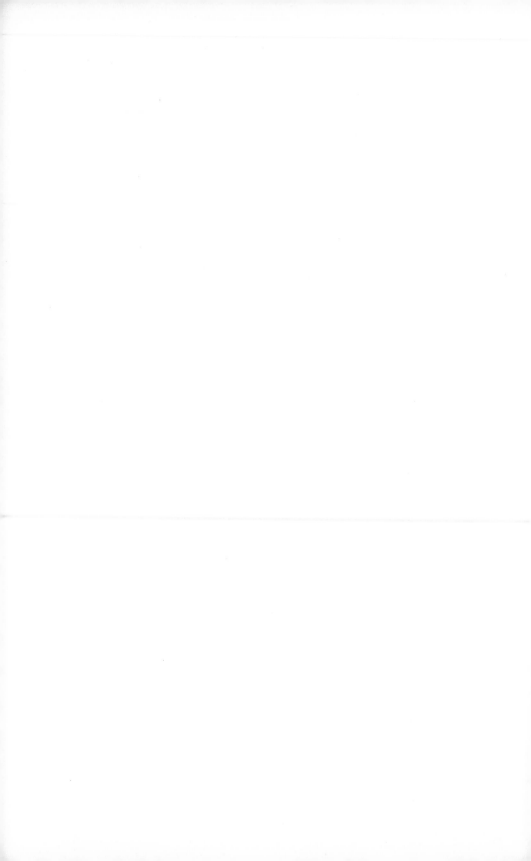

FOREWORD

WE WHO HAVE for years admired Helen Rowe Henze's poetic gift, as shown in her previous volumes of poetry, have noticed in contemporary periodicals an occasional daring translation of a Horatian Ode in its metre, foreign to English verse. We may have considered these only as talented tours de force. Now we have before us the entire corpus of the Odes in those ancient measures and suddenly realize that in an age devoted to rhythm—African, Caribbean, native American jazz—she has made a most timely demonstration of how Greco-Roman poetic rhythm may be accommodated to modern ears, and has thereby given some idea of the effect produced on Horace's contemporaries in a period strikingly like our own in rhythmical experimentation.

That this may be adorned with poetic grace and charm is Mrs. Henze's superb achievement. It raises her to the undisputed rank of a literary innovator of whom we Americans may be justly proud. Knowing personally of the toilsome hours of patient search for the right word or phrase to reproduce the poet's thought in the rhythm and the inspiration of the original Latin—an achievement also on Horace's part, for they were foreign also to his language—I salute her for a *monumentum aere perennius* in double meaning.

Some medieval composer discovered that Horace's "Integer vitae," although written in quantitative metre, sings perfectly in our modern accentual pronunciation. In like manner Helen Rowe Henze has proved, as in Book III, Ode 27, that charming English poetry may be written in the immortal measures taken over here by Horace from Sappho.

CHARLES UPSON CLARK

New York City

PREFACE

Two thousand years have not dimmed the freshness, vigor, delicacy, and charm of the Odes of Horace. Generation after generation discovers them anew with delighted wonder. The elusive charm of Horace lies not only in *what* he says, but in *how* he says it. The thirteen metres which Horace borrowed from the Greek poets for his own Odes he adapted to the Latin tongue with consummate artistry, embellishing them with all the rhetorical devices of which the language and the poetic forms were capable: interlocked word order, repetition of a word at the beginning of successive lines or phrases for dramatic emphasis, repetition of a word at the end of a line or in the body of a passage for emotional intensity, juxtaposition of contradictory words, the binding of a sentence or clause by widely separated words which agree grammatically—these and other poetic devices, placed with artistic care into the metrical requirements, produced a mosaic of color and beauty untranslatable into another tongue.

Translation of the Odes of Horace has tempted many poets to their undoing; so much has been lost in the transference of poetic values. In prose translations the lilt of the poetry is lost, even though accuracy is sometimes attained. In poetic translations into English metres using end-rhyme, accuracy has often been sacrificed to poetic necessity; the essential spirit has disappeared. An occasional trans-

ix

lator has creditably translated a few of the Odes into English using the original metres; but, to the best of my knowledge and the most reliable information I have been able to obtain, a complete translation of the Odes into English in the original metres has never before been made. That I should have been selected, as it were, to make one is to me quite as astonishing as it no doubt will be to the sharpest critics of my work.

The translation presented seemingly insuperable difficulties; however, in some miraculous way, the problems of trying to be accurate, grammatical, rhetorical, and metrical all at the same time were in most cases solved. In addition to all this, there was the necessity of conveying the elegance, the ineluctable Horatian essence, so that the reader of English could catch something of what the reader of Latin finds so enchanting in these priceless lines. I have noted at the foot of each ode the respective metrical scheme, and a brief explanation of the individual metrical systems will be found in the Appendix.

I wish to acknowledge with grateful thanks my debt to D. Herbert Abel, professor of classical languages in Loyola University of Chicago, who persuaded me to undertake this translation, and whose counsel was a never-ending source of inspiration and encouragement. My thanks also go to Charles Upson Clark, former professor of Latin in Yale University, onetime director of the classical school of the American Academy in Rome, and more recently head of New York City College until his retirement, who graciously gave me many valuable suggestions.

I have done my best. Doubtless I could continue indefinitely making small alterations and substitutions here and there, and at the end might still feel that something had escaped me from the original. Although fully aware of the translation's imperfections, I feel that, insofar as my capabilities extend, the work is finished. I release the book to the reader's charity and, I hope, enjoyment.

July 13, 1961   HELEN ROWE HENZE
Kansas City, Missouri

ACKNOWLEDGMENTS

CERTAIN OF THESE TRANSLATIONS have appeared in the following publications, to which grateful acknowledgment is made for permission to republish: *The Canadian Forum, The Cresset, The Dalhousie Review, The Fiddlehead, Kansas Magazine, New Mexico Quarterly,* and *The Step Ladder.*

During the long labor required for the final polishing of the translations presented in this volume, earlier versions of a few of them appeared also in various issues of *The Husk* and *The University of Kansas City Review.*

H. R. H.

TABLE OF CONTENTS

THE ODES OF HORACE

HORACE: HIS LIFE — HIS WORKS

QUINTUS HORATIUS FLACCUS WAS BORN on December 8, 65 B. C., at Venusia, a Roman military colony near the heel of Italy, and has never died. The *Non omnis moriar,* "I shall not wholly die," of Book III, Ode 30, in which he prophesies his immortality, has passed the test of the second millennium.

His father was a freed man, or "manumitted slave"; his mother is never mentioned, and it can only be presumed that she died when Horace was very young. In the face of class-conscious, imperial Roman society, Horace never made any attempt to conceal his lowly origin. He stated it calmly, and then proceeded to the work of building his enduring monument. Venusia was near the borders of the provinces of Apulia and Lucania, and Horace himself says he is not certain whether he is an Apulian or a Lucanian. His father may have been captured as a "slave" during a raid from one of these provinces, or he may have been taken prisoner during the civil commotions of Italy, or possibly by pirates at sea. At any rate, after saving a little money and procuring his freedom, the father seems to have prospered in his profession of *coactor*, a collector of taxes (or possibly of the proceeds of public sales), to the extent that he acquired a small estate near Venusia and was able to send his son, whose abilities were obvious at an early age, to Rome where he acquired the best education which that city afforded.

3

Horace, born after his father's emancipation, was technically *ingenuus*, freeborn. At Rome he pursued the usual courses in grammar and rhetoric, and read the older Latin poets under the tutelage of L. Orbilius Pupillus, whom he has immortalized by the epithet *plagosus*, that is, "fond of flogging." He also read Homer at this time, and studied to perfect his knowledge of Greek, of which, as a southern Italian, he probably already possessed some knowledge. He even composed some Greek verses which he later destroyed. Yet throughout his life he retained his devotion to the Greek models, and his proudest accomplishment was that he was able to bring the Greek poetic metres over into the Latin tongue by his use of them in his own poetry.

At about the age of twenty, he went to study at Athens, which was in the nature of a finishing school for young Romans of the better class. There his days were pleasant and his studies enjoyable. He was by temperament an Epicurean, but the lofty morality and discipline of the Stoics drew him as they did many others of the great Romans, and his writings contain many allusions to Stoic doctrines and paradoxes. At Athens, too, he probably studied for the first time Archilochus, Alcaeus, Sappho, and the Greek lyric poets whose characteristic poetic metres he used later in the Odes and Epodes. But upon this calm and sequestered existence broke the news of the assassination of Julius Caesar, in 44 B.C.; and in the civil wars which followed, he, with many of the young Roman nobility, joined the party of Brutus and Cassius against the triumvirs. In spite of his youth and humble birth, he was given the position of military tribune; and he accompanied the republican army through Macedonia and Thessaly and on into Asia. He returned to Macedonia in the autumn of 42 B.C.; and, after the defeat of the army at Philippi before the forces of Octavius and Mark Antony, he escaped and returned to Italy. There he found his father dead and his little inheritance confiscated for the use of the veterans of the victorious triumvirs.

The next few years were the most difficult of Horace's life. He took to writing verses to make a little money, and perhaps he hoped to attract a wealthy patron. To support himself he procured a modest clerkship in the Treasury, which he may have bought with borrowed money or obtained through the influence of his father's friends. The writing of the Epodes and Satires occupied him during the next decade. His verses won him the friendship of Vergil and Varius, the rising poets of the age, who in 39 B.C., introduced him to Maecenas, the great prime minister of Octavius Caesar Augustus. This was the beginning of an admiration and friendship between Maecenas and Horace which was to endure for the remainder of their lives. From this time forth, Horace's path was smoothed. Maecenas presented him with a small estate, the famous Sabine farm, about thirty miles from Rome and beautifully situated in the valley of the Digentia among the Sabine Hills, about fourteen miles beyond Tibur. Horace refers to this with gratitude and modesty, telling of the frugality of his table and the simplicity of his life, yet stating his confidence that, if he were to want more, his powerful friend would not withhold it. When we remember, however, that this lovely little estate employed eight slaves and that there were also five tenant-farms attached to it, perhaps we may take with a grain of salt Horace's comments on the modesty of his circumstances.

About 35 B.C., Horace published the first book of Satires, and some five years later, the second book of Satires and the Epodes. In 23 B.C. he collected and published, with a dedication to Maecenas, the first three books of the Odes. Three or four years later the first book of the Epistles was published. These consisted of twenty little letters of friendship or moral essays varying in length from about twenty to one hundred lines of verse. They are models of refinement, kindly good sense, and gentle worldly wisdom. Horace's frank but dignified acceptance of the Empire had won for him the favor of Augustus, who offered him both his personal friendship and the post of confidential secretary. "Treat me quite freely," wrote the Emperor in a letter quoted by Suetonius, "as if you were my intimate friend. You will be quite correct in this, and not at all presumptuous, since I myself have wished this to be your attitude toward me, if it can be done with due regard to your welfare." Horace gratefully accepted the friendship, but with sturdy independence rejected the position as secretary. He was a patriot, as his great political odes prove; his maxim *Dulce et decorum est pro patria mori* was a simple, unornamented statement of his own philosophy; Rome was the great love of his life, yet he was not a politician. He preferred the quiet life of a country gentleman, the sylvan simplicity of the Sabine Hills. The Emperor, with wisdom and understanding, accepted his decision; yet Alfred Noyes in his book *Horace: A Portrait* states, "There is one sentence, curiously self-revealing in a later letter from Augustus: 'Why is it that you avoid addressing me of all men in your poems? Is it that you are afraid posterity will think the worse of you for having been a friend of mine?' "[1] This desire of the Emperor to be sung was to bear fruit later.

Although Horace had served against him under Brutus at Philippi and had never publicly recanted or paid any direct tribute to the new regime, Augustus was both magnanimous and shrewd. He wished to draw what was left of the Republican tradition into the service of the Empire; and, in the process of fulfilling this plan of strengthening his own regime, it was the powerful emperor, and not the relatively helpless poet, who held out his hand in supplication. In 17 B.C., Augustus commissioned Horace to write the Carmen Saeculare, that is, the song in celebration of the Secular Games. The *ludi saeculares* were traditionally celebrated at the expiration of a long period (under Augustus it was 110 years), and constituted a religious festival of tremendous splendor and importance. It lasted for three days.

To quote again from Alfred Noyes:

The celebration of 17 B.C. went far beyond the proclamation of the heralds. It not only surpassed what any living man

[1] (New York, 1947), 9.

6

had seen; it was by far the most magnificent religious festival in the history of pre-Christian Rome—the richest in color, ritual, and poetry, and all that could appeal to the imagination; the most stirring in its national aspirations; the most moving in the deeper and largely unconscious implications of its prayers to the gods from the heights of the Capitol and the Palatine.

On the third day of the celebration, in the culminating act of worship and supplication, the *Carmen Saeculare* was sung by a choir of twenty-seven young men and twenty-seven girls. A certain divine significance was attached to these multiples of three and nine. The hymn for this occasion has justified its author's belief that his works would prove to be more durable than bronze or marble; but, as Professor Rand observed, in his fine book *The Building of Eternal Rome*: "Many a modern friend of Horace has visited the Museo delle Terme to pay his respects to certain slabs of marble there, on which in beautiful Augustan capitals fragments of the official account of the *ludi saeculares* have been preserved. The words that this traveler seeks first of all read: *Carmen composuit Q. Horatius Flaccus*."

The composition of the Carmen Saeculare was probably the greatest single event of Horace's life. In spite of his gentle independence, his repeated insistence throughout his writings that he was a writer of light lyrics, not a narrator of epic themes; that he had not the sweep nor scope of Pindar with his magnificent irregular rhythms; that he himself worked painstakingly, laboriously like the "Matine bee" (IV, 2) on the intricate elaboration of his smaller verses—in spite of this he had consented at last to place his lyre at the service of his patrons. He who had once prided himself on the selectness of his audience now revelled in the sunshine of popular adulation. He occupied a quasi-official position as poet laureate of the court of Augustus. His fame was now securely established, and he felt that his chief work had been done. He had felt this even earlier, upon the publication of the first three books of the Odes, the last of which, Ode 30 of Book III, is in the nature of an epilogue, beginning *Exegi monumentum aere perennius*, "I have completed a monument more enduring than bronze."

It was later, and mainly at the request of the Emperor, that he began the composition of the fourth book of the Odes. He begins with the exquisitely beautiful, nostalgic love lyric:

> *Intermissa, Venus, diu*
>   *Rursus bella moves? Parce, precor, precor.*
> *Non sum qualis eram bonae*
>   *Sub regno Cinarae.*

"Venus, after so long a truce/ Do you now move to war? Spare me, I pray, I pray!/ I am not the same man I was/ In sweet Cinara's reign."

This fourth book contains the laureate odes written to commemorate the victories of Augustus' stepsons, Drusus and Tiberius. It also contains some of the loveliest lines Horace ever wrote: the beautiful *Diffugere nives* (IV, 7), "Now are the snows all fled, and the grass returns to the fields/ Tresses return to trees"; (IV, 8), "I would give to my friends goblets of cherished bronze"; the preparations for a little party in honor of Maecenas' birthday (IV, 11), "Alban wine, a caskful, I have here, Phyllis."

The second book of the Epistles completes the list of Horace's works. This comprised three long essays in hexameter verse on matters of literary criticism and taste. The first, addressed to Augustus and called forth by his specific request, was a commentary on the state of poetic taste at Rome. The second was the epistle to Florus, and the third the epistle to the Pisos, a father and his two sons who wanted to write plays and poetry, and who had written to Horace, asking for advice. They were lacking in talent, but Horace was too kind to say so. He did point out, however, that mediocrity in poetry cannot be tolerated, and advised the elder son to show his work to a competent critic, then to lock it up for nine years so that he might have the opportunity of destroying it later on while it was still unseen by the world. Then he proceeded to a general discussion of poetry and its pitfalls. This epistle has come to be known as the "*Ars Poetica*," or "The Art of Poetry."

Horace's charm endures. He holds us even now because his wit, his melancholy, and his tender gaiety include us. He is today the same gentle, urbane, sophisticated, gay, contented, disillusioned, adroit, endearing companion that he was for his own circle of friends two thousand years ago, the friends who were second in his affections only to his unswerving loyalty to Rome. He loved to have people in, to entertain with small, modest dinner parties at his Sabine farm, serving wine produced on his own estate, bottled perhaps by his own hand—unpretentious repasts, but where the silver saltcellar was kept shining.

Horace never married. He was certainly not indifferent to women, but the amatory odes display no great depth of passion; even in the tenderest there is a light touch. His great emotions were centered elsewhere, and even there they were kept under control. Control, restraint, balance, a delicate sense of the fitness of things; these were the motivating characteristics which made Horace the man and the poet that he was. Yet the various women who flit through Horace's Odes doubtless had, at least in some instances, human prototypes: the lovely Cinara; the shy, fawnlike Chloe; the spirited Lydia; the flirtatious Pyrrha; the heartless Barina; coy Lydia with the ivory lyre, her hair in a knot like a Spartan maiden's. Horace knew the game of love, and played it like a gentleman. Cinara was probably real; as for the rest, whether real or not, we cannot identify them. Nor does it matter; it is not always necessary for a poet to be in love with his originals. The quality of his affection was for friendship rather than for love, and he set as high a value on it as any Epicurean. More than thirty men, including the greatest names of the Augustan age, as well as a number of others who would have been known to us from other sources, were the recipients of odes or epistles from Horace. In a few cases, the individual's sole claim to immortality is that he was mentioned by Horace.

Horace had his troubles, however. He was disappointed in the reception accorded the publication of the first three books of the Odes. Already, in 24 B.C., Quintilius Varus, his friend and critic, had died. But there was worse to come: a breach between Maecenas and Augustus. Late in 23 B.C. a conspiracy against Augustus was nipped in the bud, but the news leaked out to friends of the conspirators. This leak was traced to the beautiful Terentia, wife of Maecenas, in whom he had confided. Terentia was a half-sister of Licinius Murena, one of those executed for complicity in the plot. There was no question of dismissing Maecenas, for the knight held no official position at court. The breach was healed on the surface; but Maecenas was no longer important, and he must have felt it deeply. In the year 19 B.C., Horace lost two more of his friends, Vergil and Tibullus. It was from this depression that Augustus' commission in 17 B.C. to write the Carmen Saeculare rescued him, and gave him a new lease on life.

In physical characteristics and temperament, Horace describes himself as small in stature, prematurely gray, and in middle age tending toward plumpness. He admits to being quick-tempered, but was quick to get over his anger. He hints that when the dark locks clustered above his low forehead, he needed no further recommendations to the favor of the fair.

Notwithstanding Horace's wit, humor, urbanity, and worldly wisdom, he had a very strong moral sense. He was always interested in human conduct, and the humanity of his philosophy was evidenced not only by the sincerity of his affection for his friends but by his concern (in an age not greatly troubled by such things) over the plight of the poor and the friendless. He pictures with pity in Book II, Ode 18, the evicted peasant family, husband and wife, driven forth with their ragged children and clutching in their garments their ancestral gods. Even in the bantering ode to Iccius, Book I, Ode 29, he asks with compassionate insight:

> What strange, what savage, barbarous maiden then,
> Her lover slain, will serve and attend your wants;
>   What royal page with locks anointed
>   Stand as your cupbearer close beside you,

Who once was taught the Serican arrow's aim
From father's bowstring?

It must have been an interesting inner adventure for Horace when he began to discover in the quietude of the Sabine farm that he found himself believing more and more definitely in a Supreme Power. The first evidence of this in his writings is in Book I, Ode 34, when the "clap of thunder" out of a clear sky convinced him that there is a Mind manifesting itself in the universe and controlling the destinies of man. Noyes comments:

> The "clap of thunder" is not to be taken literally, of course; but neither is it to be taken "playfully," as one famous critic would have it. . . . It is sometimes said that Horace was "converted" from Epicureanism to Stoicism, but this is not quite true; for, as we have seen—he had never bound himself to any school of philosophy. He would take from any, or all of them, whatever seemed necessary to his scheme of thought, and he would discard the rest of their doctrine with a gay and impartial smile. It was not necessarily a smile at the tenets of the philosophers. . . . The gentleness with which he touches the old Italian religion of the field and fold—as in the prayer to Faunus—was due to his instinctive sense that these personifications were attempts of the human mind to represent the various attributes of a single divine Power, manifested throughout the universe.

It seems evident from Horace's writings that he was aware of a divine protection. He described in Book III, Ode 4, how when he was a little lost child in the forests of Apulia and, spent with play, he lay asleep and the drifting leaves covered him, he felt sure it was the birds that had concealed him from bears and deadly vipers. There was the wolf that turned and left him unharmed as he was wandering through the Sabine Hills, composing an ode to Lalage (I, 22); there was the falling tree that grazed but did not hurt him (II, 13). The propitious eye of Melpomene watched over the hour of his birth, and in the lovely Ode 3 of Book IV, Horace gives thanks to the Muse to whom he owes his inspiration and his power to please. Simplicity, moderation, and good humour characterized his life and thought; yet he took a human pride in the fact that passers-by in the street pointed him out as "player of the Roman lyre."

Mackail, in his *Latin Literature* comments aptly on the Horatian Odes: "Before a volume of which every other line is as familiar as a proverb criticism is almost silenced."[2] In Horace's writings there is no really profound thought and no great intensity of feeling. His themes are the Epicurean and Stoic commonplaces, graceful verse exercises modeled after the Greek, the noble but not exciting patriotic Odes, tributes to friendship, the dignified recognition of Augustus as the restorer of peace to the troubled state. The love poems are light; his humour, gentle. The quality of his style consists mainly in the exquisite art with which he fashions the commonplace into a jewel-like setting which transforms an everyday philosophy into small gems which gleam with the light of poetic feeling, restraint, pathos, intelligence, modesty, and a lively wit that flashes sympathetically over the idiosyncrasies and the lot of man. He tells us that the bloom of the rose is brief, that good wine makes for good fellowship but must be used moderately, that pallid death pounds with impartial foot at huts of the poor and rich men's mansions, that we cannot escape ourselves, that the golden mean is best, that black care sits behind the horseman, that it is sweet and proper to die for the fatherland, that he who governs his own nature is stronger than he who sits on the throne of Cyrus. And when Horace has said it, the thing crystallizes in our minds as the only possible way the point could have been made and made so well.

All of this is the more striking when one considers the comparative poverty of the Latin vocabulary. In contrast to the richness of the Greek compound epithets capable of expressing infinite variety and shades of meaning, the Latin vocabulary range is limited, plain, almost bare.

[2] (New York, 1900), 112.

To compensate for the parsimony of the language, Horace resorted to several devices to give color to his poetry: explicit personification and the use of allegory, capitalized abstraction, and the suggestion of life and personality by the use of epithet or verb. He also employed with an illuminating effect the use of proper names laden with associations of history, mythology, literature, and geographical locations. Without overloading his style, Horace carefully chose just those names calculated to arouse pleasant associations in the mind of the average, educated man. Mr. Paul Shorey's cataloguing of examples is to the point:

> The sea is Hadrian, Cretic, Icarian, Carpathian, Aegean, Tyrrhenian, Apulian, or Caspian. Merchandise is Tyrian, Cyprian, or Bithynian. Purple is Laconian, Phrygian, Numidian, or Hymettian. Riches are the wealth of Attalus or Achaemenes, of India, or the unspoiled treasures of Araby. The ship is the Pontic pine or the Bithynian keel. A mountain is stark Niphates or black-wooded Erymanthus. Snow is Sithonian, the harrow Sabine, the pruning hook Calenian, the harvest Sardinian or African, the feast Sicilian, the bee Calabrian, the lyric song Aeolian, the dirge Simonidean or Cean, the lute Teian, the buskin Cecropian, the laurel Apolline, Delphic or Delian, the poison Colchian or Thessalian, the pipe Berecynthian, the sword Norican, the coat of mail Iberian, the lioness Gaetulian, the threshing floor Licyan. A dangerous strait is Bosphorus or the waters that pour between the glittering Cyclades; astrology is Babylonian numbers; ointment is Achaemenian nard or Syrian malabathron; a storm is the tumult of the Aegean; athletics is the Olympic dust, the Isthmian labor or the Elean palm.[3]

Horace takes the thin, barren, Latin vocabulary and by his skill in handling it, by the images he conjures up, and by the use of proper names carrying pictures in themselves, he creates surprising effects of concreteness and sensuous beauty. And finally, by bringing the Greek metrical measures over into the Latin, he created a variety of musical effects hitherto unknown in Latin poetry.

[3] *Horace—Odes and Epodes* (Boston, 1910), xxiv.

Blest by the gods he was, and fortunate in the human relation-
ships which smoothed his path. These he accepted with dignity,
grace, and gratitude. His devotion to Maecenas endured. Horace
assured his friend that their horoscopes coincided and that he felt
that by the will of Heaven their two lives were bound together. During an illness of Maecenas, Horace addressed to him Ode 17 of
Book II:

> Why, why with your complaints do you slay my soul?
> No pleasure to the gods, neither will of mine
>   Is it that you die first, Maecenas,
>   Glory and pillar of all my substance.
>
> Ah then, if sudden death snatches you, my life's
> Best part, why should the rest of me linger on,
>   Since not content nor whole would I live
>   After you? That day will bring destruction
>
> To both. For I have sworn the not-faithless oath,
> The soldier's oath, that thus we shall go, shall go
>   As soon as you pass on before me,
>   Comrades prepared for that last, long journey.

In the year 8 B.C., Maecenas died. He left his great palace on
the Esquiline, with all his art treasures and all his wealth, to Augustus; and he left him another legacy, an imperishable one which
has overshadowed all the rest in the memory of men, one sentence:
Horati Flacci ut mei esto memor, "Remember Horatius Flaccus as
you would remember me."

But there was not much time. Within a few months, up the
Esquiline Hill to be buried near Maecenas, was borne the dust of
that body which was at best only the shadow of Horace.

BOOK I

"We are asked for song." — I, 32

Maecenas,[1] from your royal sires so lately sprung,
O protection of mine, glory so sweet to me,
Those there are who enjoy gath'ring Olympic[2] dust,
Glowing chariot wheels grazing the turning post;
They take pride in the palm branch which ennobles them,
Lifts them up to the gods, lords of the earth are they;
One is pleased if the mob, fickle still though it be,
Triple honors shall give, fighting to raise him up;
That one wishes to store safe in his waiting barn
Grain swept up from the floor, threshings of Libyan[3] wheat.
One who joyously hoes ancestral plots of ground
You could not, though on terms granted by Attalus,[4]
Could not ever persuade, borne in a Cyprian bark,
(Timid sailor!) to go ploughing the Myrtoan[5] Sea.
Fearing African wind wrestling Icarian waves,
Peace the trader commends, rest, and the fields of home;
Soon he mends all his boats, boats which were dashed and tossed,
Since he cannot endure poverty, suffering.
One there is who spurns not goblets of Massic wine,
Nor to take for himself part of the business day,
Limbs stretched out at his ease under a flowering shrub
Or where some sacred stream springs at its fountainhead.
Warlike camps delight some, sound of the trumpet's blare
Mixed with clarion notes, battles which mothers hate.
Under skies that are cold, patient the hunter waits,
All things else he forgets, even his tender wife,
Hoping deer will be seen soon by his faithful dogs,
Or a Marsian[6] boar burst through the twisted nets.
Me, the scholars' rewards, garlands of ivy leaves,

Make as one with the gods, crowning my head and brow.
Me, the cool grove and nymphs dancing with satyrs there
Set apart from the crowd, far from the populace,
If Euterpe⁷ her flutes never withholds, nor does
Polyhymnia⁸ shun tuning the Lesbian lyre.
If with poets you place me in the lyric choir,
With my head raised so high, then shall I strike the stars!⁹

¹ Gaius Cilinius Maecenas, 70?–8 B.C., the wealthy first minister under Augustus, patron of Horace, Vergil, and Propertius, was in large measure the architect of Augustan administration.

² The Olympic Games were the most famous of the national festivals of Greece. They were held every fourth year at Olympia.

³ Libya, in North Africa, was the chief source of Rome's grain supply.

⁴ The wealth of the Attalids, kings of Pergamon in Asia Minor, was proverbial.

⁵ The western Aegean.

⁶ The country of the Marsi, a mountainous district in the center of Italy, abounded in game.

⁷ The Muse of music.

⁸ One of the Muses.

⁹ Metre: First Asclepiadean.

Now enough of snow and portentous hailstorms
Jove has sent to earth and, with red hand hurling
Bolts against our temple-crowned sacred hilltops,
    Frightened the city,

Frightened nations, lest there come back upon us
Pyrrha's[1] burdened age and prodigious happenings,
As when Proteus[2] drove his whole herd up to
    Visit the mountains.

Shoals of fishes hung in the highest elm tree
Which had long been known as the haunt of pigeons,
While, submerged and trembling, the deer bewildered
    Swam in the waters.

We have seen the waves of the yellow Tiber,
Violently flung from Etruscan shore lines,[3]
Overwhelm the monument of the king and
    Temple of Vesta,

While the doting stream, to complaining Ilia,[4]
Vaunts himself too great an avenger, as he
Overflows his left bank and sweeps beyond, to
    Jove's disapproval.

Youths will hear it, thinned by their parents' folly,
Hear how fellow-citizens sharpened broadswords,
They will hear of battles wherein the Persians
    Better had perished.

Which god now, which god shall the people call to
Save this empire rushing to ruin? How with
Prayer shall sacred virgins[5] petition Vesta,
    Deaf to their chanting?

Now to whom will Jupiter give the role, the
Part of expiating our crimes? We pray you,
Come with cloak of cloud on your shining shoulders,
    Seer Apollo;

Or, may you come, Venus, the laughter-loving,
You whom Jocus[6] hovers about and Cupid;
Or if you, our founder, behold your race,[7] your
    Sons so neglected,

Cloyed with sport, alas! far too long continued,
You whom noise delights and the smooth war helmets,
Glare of unhorsed Moor at his bloodstained foeman,
    Fierce and unyielding;

Or, if you, winged son[8] of the gentle Maia,
Having changed your form, show a young man's figure
Here on earth, while letting yourself be known as
    Caesar's avenger,

Late be your return to the heavenly regions,
Long your happy stay with Quirinus' people,[9]
Not impatient over our faults, and may no
    Breezes untimely

Bear you off; for here even greater triumphs
May you love, called Father and Chief, nor shall the
Medes, unpunished, ride on their raids—not while you[10]
    Lead us, O Caesar![11]

1 Rome and mankind feared a return of the flood, of which Deucalion and his wife Pyrrha were the only survivors.

2 Proteus, a sea god, kept Neptune's herd, i.e., seals.

3 By Etruscan shore lines is meant the coast of Italy from the mouth of the Tiber northward. Some authorities take it to mean the high right bank of the Tiber.

4 Ilia, or Rhea Silvia, the mother of Romulus and Remus by Mars, was sometimes called the bride of the Tiber.

5 Virgins: vestal virgins. Vesta is offended by the assassination of Julius Caesar, the Pontifex Maximus.

6 Jocus, the god of sportive mirth.

7 Romulus was the son of Mars by Ilia, and so the Romans were his descendants.

8 Mercury.

9 The deified Romulus was identified with the old god Quirinus; so Quirinus' people were the Romans.

10 Octavian, Caesar Augustus.

11 Metre: Sapphic Strophe.

So may Cyprus's goddess[1] strong,
    So may stars shining bright, Helen's twin brothers[2] there,
May the sire of the winds so rule—
    Having bound them all up, all except Iapyx[3]—that
You bring Vergil unharmed, O ship,
    Now entrusted to you, safe to the shores of Greece.
Oh, deliver him safe and sound,
    Who is half of my soul! Watch over him I pray.
'Round the heart of him who was first
    To consign his frail craft out on the savage sea
Oak and triply laid brass were bound,
    Neither feared he the wind headlong from Africa
Fighting blasts of Aquilo,[4] nor
    Feared the Hyades'[5] gloom, neither mad Notus' rage
Who is tyrant of Adria[6]
    If he wishes to raise, or to calm down, the waves.
How could he have feared death's dread step
    Who beheld with dry eyes monsters which swam the deep,
Gazed on turbulent, swelling tides,
    Saw those infamous rocks, Acroceraunia?
Vainly then in His wisdom God
    Separated the lands, sundering them by seas,
If our impious boats go through,
    Leap the not-to-be touched billows prohibited.
Boldly daring to suffer all,
    Mankind rushes ahead into forbidden crime.
Boldly Iapetus' son[7] brought fire
    By a mischievous fraud, down to the tribes on earth.
After theft of the fire from heaven,

Wasting sickness appeared, brooding upon the lands,
And a new throng of fevers lay;
    Unavoidable death, once far away and slow-
Moving, quickened its lagging step.
    Skillful Daedalus[8] tried braving the airy void
Although wings were not given to man;
    While great Hercules' task plunged him to Acheron.[9]
By men nothing is deemed too hard,
    And in folly we reach even for heaven itself;
Nor do we by our sins permit
    Angry Jove to lay down thunderbolts of his wrath.[10]

[1] Venus.

[2] Castor and Pollux, forming the constellation Gemini, were appealed to in time of peril at sea.

[3] Iapyx was the west-northwest wind, and favorable to those sailing from Italy to Greece.

[4] Aquilo, the north wind.

[5] Hyades, the "rain stars."

[6] The Adriatic Sea.

[7] Iapetus' son, Prometheus, stole fire from heaven and brought it to men in a hollow reed.

[8] An Athenian who made wax wings for himself and his son Icarus.

[9] Acheron, one of the rivers of Hades, is used here for Hades itself.

[10] Metre: Second Asclepiadean.

23

With sweet return of the spring and Favonius,[1] winter is relaxing,
    And rollers draw down thirsty ships for launching,
Now does the herd find no joy in the stalls, nor the plowman in his hearth fire.
    No longer are the meadows white with hoarfrost.
Under the moon overhanging, Cythera's[2] own Venus leads the dances
    As hand in hand the nymphs and comely Graces
Stamp on the earth, one foot after the other, while glowing Vulcan visits
    The ponderous forges of the giant Cyclops.[3]
Now it is fitting to wreathe with green myrtle one's shining head—or else with
    The flowers which the loosened earth is bearing,
And in the shady groves make now our dutiful sacrifice to Faunus,[4]
    Should he demand a lamb, perchance a kidling.
Pallid death pounds with impartial foot ports of the poor and rich men's mansions.
    O Sestius, you blessed son of fortune,
Life's so brief span thus forbids us to undertake hopes that stretch out too long.
    Soon night will close on you, the fabled spirits,
Presently Pluto's[5] bleak kingdom will crowd you; and, once departed thither,
    You will not cast for sovereignty of revels,
Nor at the beauty of Lycidas[6] marvel in whom all youth is glowing,
    For whom the maids will soon grow warm a little.[7]

[1] Favonius, also called Zephyrus, was the west wind.
[2] An island in the Aegean Sea, celebrated for the worship of Venus.
[3] Three giant sons of Uranus and Gaea.
[4] The protecting deity of flocks, herds, and agriculture.
[5] Pluto was the god of the lower world.
[6] The name of this youth is probably fictitious.
[7] Metre: Fourth Archilochian.

I, 5

Ah, what delicate lad sprinkled with liquid scents
Now on many a rose pleads with you, Pyrrha,[1] there
    In some favorite grotto?
       Now for whom do you bind, so trim,

Your bright red-golden hair? How oft, alas! will he
Weep your changed faith, changed gods! Marveling, he will gaze
    At seas roughened by black winds,
       Staring, stunned by the strange, new sight,

Who, believing you gold, feels now but joy in you,
Who now hopes you'll be sweet, pleasant, and fancy-free;
    He knows naught of your false breeze,
       Shifting, treacherous! Wretched, they

For whom, untried, you shine. Me—well, the sacred wall
In a votive scene shows, plain on my tablet,[2] that
    To the sea's mighty god, long
       Since I hung up my dripping clothes.[3]

[1] Pyrrha (a fictitious name) means reddish-yellow, the fashionable color.
[2] Sailors who had suffered shipwreck were accustomed to dedicate to Neptune or Isis some sort of tablet or picture commemorating the event, together with the clothes they had worn at the time.
[3] Metre: Fourth Asclepiadean.

By winged Varius[1] then, bird of Homeric song,
Shall your exploits be sung, victor o'er enemies,
Deeds with you as the chief, bold both with ships and horse,
    Truly these will he celebrate.

We, Agrippa,[2] cannot venture to sing of them!
Neither sing we of war nor of Achilles' wrath,
Nor the course through the sea wily Ulysses took,
    Neither Pelops' fierce, cruel house.[3]

These we shall not attempt, shame and the Muse forbid
Since the singer is weak; great is the song, nor should
Praise of Caesar and you fall to the peaceful lyre,
    Or be lessened by lack of art.

Who but Varius could worthily tell of Mars
Wrapped in tunic of bronze, or black with dust of Troy
Picture Meriones,[4] or by Athena's aid
    Diomedes[5] at one with gods?

We shall sing of the feasts, we'll sing of angry maids
As they battle with youths, scratching with short-cut nails;
Whether free be our heart, whether we burn with love,
    Lightly, as is our wont, we sing![6]

---

[1] L. Varius, friend of Horace and Vergil, was after Vergil, the chief epic poet of the day.

[2] M. Vipsanius Agrippa was the right hand of Augustus in war, as Maecenas was in peace.

3 The history of the house of Pelops, father of Atreus and Thyestes, and grand-father of Agamemnon and Menelaus, was used many times as the subject for tragedies.

4 Meriones was the charioteer of the Cretan Idomeneus.

5 Diomedes, urged on by Pallas, wounded Ares and Aphrodite in the Trojan War.

6 Metre: Third Asclepiadean.

Others will praise sunny Rhodes, Mytilene, or Ephesus,[1] singing
    Ramparts of Corinth with seas double-harbored,
Thebes long renowned for her Bacchus,[2] or Delphi because of Apollo,
    Or, perhaps Thessaly's valley of Tempe.
Some have one topic, to celebrate always the city of Pallas,
    Endlessly singing its praises, and thus to
Place on their brows a fine wreath of the olive they culled from all quarters.
    Many a poet in honor of Juno
Fitly will tell of the horses of Argos, the wealth of Mycenae.
    Me, neither Sparta, the hardy, affected,
Nor did the fields of the fertile Larisa[3] impress with their beauty
    More than Albunea's[4] echoing grotto,
More than the freshets of Anio[5] falling, the grove there at Tibur,
    Orchards all damp with the swift-flowing streamlets.
Often the whitening wind from the south wipes the clouds from the dark sky,
    Not always does it bring rainstorm and tempest;
Therefore be wise and remember, O Plancus,[6] no need for dejection,
    Mellowing wine soon will end all your troubles,
Whether in gleaming camps under bright standards, or whether at Tibur
    Dense shade shall hold you. When Teucer,[7] an exile,
Fled from his fatherland, fled forth from Salamis, yet was he moved when
    Starting his journey, despite all his woe, to
Bind round his temples a poplar wreath sprinkled with wine, the releaser,
    Speaking to all his sad friends words of comfort:
"Comrades and friends, now wherever our fortunes, more kind than my father,
    Hereafter lead us, we thither shall follow!
Never despair then with Teucer your leader and Teucer your seer;
    Since the unerring Apollo has sent him
Forth to dispute the old name with a new name of Salamis henceforth.

O my brave men, who so often have suffered
Worse things than these are, now drink with me, banish with wine all your sorrow;
We'll sail again 'cross the vast sea tomorrow![8]

[1] Isles of Greece.

[2] Bacchus, the god of wine and poets, was, according to the myth, born at Thebes.

[3] A town in Thessaly.

[4] The sibyl Albunea, whose grotto echoed from the sound of the cataract.

[5] Anio—the river is now called "Teverone."

[6] Plancus may have been a native of Tibur, or possibly had a villa there.

[7] Teucer, the son of Telamon of Salamis and the brother of Ajax. When he returned from the Trojan War without Ajax (who had killed himself because the arms of Achilles were awarded to Ulysses), his father drove him into exile. He sailed to Cyprus and there founded a city which is called Salamis.

[8] Metre: Alcmanian Strophe.

Lydia,[1] speak, I pray you
By the gods! Why do you ruin Sybaris like this with love?
    Why does he hate the sunny
Field of athletes, he who once bore well both the dust and sunshine?
    Why does he now not ride forth
With his peers like any soldier? Why does he not subdue the
    Mouths of the Gallic[2] steeds with
Wolf-fanged bits? And why does he fear swimming the Tiber? Why, like
    Poisonous viper's blood, does
He now shun the wrestler's oil? Nor does he carry bruised arms,
    He who could throw the discus
Past the mark, the javelin, too; once he was famous for that!
    Why is he hiding as the
Son of Thetis,[3] nymph of the sea, hid ere the fall of sad Troy,
    Lest a man's garb and lest the
Lycian allies hasten him forth into the midst of slaughter?[4]

[1] Lydia and Sybaris are perhaps symbolic of luxury and effeminacy.

[2] The horses of Gaul were noted for their spirit.

[3] Thetis, with foreknowledge of the fate that awaited her son at Troy, clothed Achilles in the garments of a maiden among the daughters of Lycomedes, king of Scyros. When the wily Odysseus placed arms among gifts offered to the girls, Achilles betrayed himself by seizing upon them.

[4] Metre: Greater Sapphic Strophe.

Behold how tall Soracte[1] looms, and how white!
No longer can the laboring forests hold
    Their snowy burden; streams are frozen,
        Locked in the grip of the piercing coldness.

Dispel the chill air, piling the great logs high
Upon the hearth; unstintingly now bring forth
    And pour the mellow, four-year vintage,
        O Thaliarchus,[2] from Sabine wine jar.

Leave to the gods the rest, for when they have stilled
The warring winds that battle upon the sea
    The cypress is no longer shaken,
        No longer vexed are the aged ash trees.

Whate'er tomorrow holds, shun to question now,
And what the day will bring, what of chance or gain,
    Set down to profit; now in boyhood
        Spurn not sweet loves or the youthful dances,

While from your bloom cantankerous age stands off.
Now 'neath the falling dusk, at the trysting hour
    Again, again through field and courtyard
        Let the soft whispers be still repeated.

Now from a secret corner a teasing laugh
Betrays a hidden girl, from whose slender wrists
   A lover's pledge is snatched away, or
      Else from a finger resisting faintly.[3]

[1] A mountain in Etruria, twenty-six miles north of Rome, and visible from it.
[2] Master of the revels; the name was probably coined by Horace.
[3] Metre: Alcaic Strophe.

Mercury,[1] O eloquent son of Atlas,
You who molded primitive men's first rough ways,
Giving them so shrewdly the gift of language,
    Patron of wrestling,

Messenger of Jove and the gods, I sing you,
You the parent god of the curving lyre,
Pleased whenever artfully as a sly joke
    Something is taken.

Once when you were young and Apollo threatened,
Frightening you to bring back the stolen oxen,
Seeing how himself was bereft of arrows,
    He fell to laughter.

Priam[2] once to Atreus'[3] sons so haughty,
Leaving Troy behind him, went rich with ransom,
When through campfires hostile to Troy you led him,
    Passed quite unnoticed.

Pious souls you place in their happy dwellings,
Curb with golden wand the pale thronging shadows,
Pleasing thus the gods of the upper regions,
    And of the lower.[4]

---

[1] Mercury was the god of eloquence and athletics, patron of thieves, wielder of the golden wand, and shepherd of the shades.

[2] Priam was a son of Laomedon, king of Troy, husband of Hecuba, and father of Hector, Helenus, Paris, Deiphobus, Cassandra, etc.; he was slain by Pyrrhus, the son of Achilles.

[3] Atreus was a son of Pelops and Hippodamia, brother of Thyestes, father of Agamemnon and Menelaus, king of Argos and Mycenae.

[4] Metre: Sapphic Strophe.

33

Dare not ever to ask, knowledge is wrong, what fate the gods have wrought
Both for me and for you, Leuconoë,[1] neither attempt to learn
Babylonian stars.[2] Better endure whate'er the fate which Jove
Has allotted to us, whether it be many more winters, or
Whether this one which breaks Tuscany's sea 'gainst the wave-hollowed rocks
Be the last. So be wise, strain now your wines; let us cut down long hope
To our life's little span. While yet we speak, jealously flees now our
Lifetime. Seize then today, trusting tomorrow no more than we must.[3]

---

[1] A fictional name.
[2] Used here to mean calculations of the Chaldean astrologers.
[3] Metre: Fifth Asclepiadean.

Man or half-god, whom do you choose to praise now,
Clio,[1] with your lyre and your fife's shrill piping?
Or what god? Whose name will be now repeated,
    Sportively echoed,

Whether heard on Helicon's[2] shaded borders,
Or on heights of Pindus[3] or frosty Haemus?[4]
Whence uprooted forests trailed blindly after
    Orpheus[5] singing,

By his mother's art he delayed the rapid
Flowing of the streams and the swift-winged breezes,
Charmed the listening oaks with his strings' sweet music,
    Leading them onward.

Whom now shall I praise before Jove the father,
He who governs men and the gods in all things,
Sea and land, the whole of the universe, and
    Changing of seasons?

Whence comes nothing greater than he himself is,
There is none like him, none to follow closely:
Next, however, honors should go to Pallas[6]
    Daring in battle;

Nor shall I be silent concerning Bacchus,
Or Diana hostile to beast, the huntress,
Neither you, O Phoebus,[7] with well-aimed arrow,
    Certain and fearful.

Hercules I sing, and the sons of Leda:[8]
One gained fame with horses, the other fighting;
When their star is sighted by timid sailors,
    Steadily beaming,

From the rocks the wind-shaken spray flows backward,
Winds die down, and clouds disappear from heaven,
Threatening waves subside in the placid ocean,
    Since they have willed it.

After these then, Romulus[9] let me mention,
Then the reign Pompilius kept so peaceful,
Tarquin's reign so splendid—I know not!—maybe
    Cato's brave dying.

I shall tell of Regulus and the Scauri
Great of spirit, prodigal Paullus also,
Tell of conqu'ring Hannibal and Fabricius
    With lofty singing.

He and unshorn Curius and Camillus,
All were bred in poverty fierce and cruel,
Fitting them for war, raised on grandsire's farmland
    In modest dwelling.

Swells Marcellus' fame like a tree grown ageless;
'Midst them all the Julian star now flashes
Like the moon among all the lesser torches,
    Gleaming eternal.

Father,[10] you who guard still the race of mankind,
Son of Saturn, now to your care is given
Caesar's fortunes; and may you reign forever,
    With Caesar second.

He will drive before him the conquered Parthians
Threatening Latium,[11] in a well-earned triumph,
Or the subject Seres[12] and Indi of the
    Orient border.

Less than you, O Jove, he will reign with justice;
You will shake Olympus with heavy chariot,
Hurling down on groves man has desecrated
    Bolts of your thunders.[13]

[1] Clio was the Muse of history.
[2] Mt. Helicon, in Boeotia, was one of the seats of worship of the Muses.
[3] Mt. Pindus, between Thessaly and Epirus, was also known for worship of the Muses.
[4] Mt. Haemus, in Thrace, was an earlier seat of the Muses.
[5] Orpheus, a legendary singer of Thrace.
[6] The goddess, Pallas Athena, was regarded in Homer as second only to Zeus in power.
[7] Apollo.
[8] Mother by Zeus of Castor and Pollux, Helen and Clytemnestra.
[9] Sqq. famous Romans.
[10] Jupiter in heaven, Augustus on earth.
[11] The region of Italy in which Rome was situated.
[12] A people of eastern Asia (the modern Chinese).
[13] Metre: Sapphic Strophe.

When you praise, O my Lydia,[1]
    Telephus' rosy neck, Telephus' wax-like arms,
Then my liver begins to burn,
    Burns and swells with my wrath, rage uncontrollable.
Neither reason remains to me
    Nor my skin's proper hue; stealthily down my cheeks
Flows a tear which betrays full well
    How completely consumed I am by sluggish fires.
I burn, whether unseemly brawls
    Caused by wine have defiled shoulders as white as snow,
Or it may be that frenzied boy
    Has pressed marks of his teeth hard on your pretty lips.
If you only would hear me through,
    You would never expect him to be constant who
Wounds so brutally that sweet mouth
    Which Venus with her own nectar has made so moist.
Three times happy and more are they
    Whom unbreakable bonds never dissolved shall hold,
Whom no quarrels shall sever, whom
    No estrangement shall part until the day of death.[2]

[1] Lydia and Telephus are fictional names.
[2] Metre: Second Asclepiadean.

I, 14

O ship,[1] seaward once more fresh waves will carry you!
Oh, what are you about? Boldly now, get to port!
    Do you not see your side bare
        And that none of your oars are there?

And your masthead is cracked, struck by swift Afric wind,
Sail yards groan, and without cables your timbers are
    Scarcely fit to withstand this
        Too imperious, surging sea!

And your sails are not whole; nor are your gods still there,
Gods on whom you will call when you are struck again;
    Pine of Pontus[2] you boast, that
        Noble daughter of noble wood,

Yet in vain is the name, vain is the lineage,
For the sailor, alarmed, trusts not to painted sterns;
    Be on guard, ship! Unless you're
        Doomed for sport with the winds, beware!

That which lately to me was but a weariness
Now is yearning and care, no light anxiety;
    Shun those waters which flow past
        The bright, glittering[3] Cyclades![4]

---

[1] The ship of state. The poem was probably written before the final establishment of the Empire.

[2] Pontus, a district on the south coast of the Black Sea, was famed for ship-timber.

[3] Cyclades: islands in the Aegean Sea lying in a circle around Delos.

[4] Metre: Fourth Asclepiadean.

When the shepherd[1] so false sailed in Idaean ships
And bore off through the straits Helen, his host's fair wife,
By an unwelcome calm, Nereus[2] stilled swift winds,
    So to sing of dread destiny:

"By an ominous bird,[3] now you are leading home
Her whom many a Greek soldier will fetch again,
Having sworn to destroy all of your marriage bonds,
    Toppling Priam's ancestral realm.

Ah, alas and alas! How great the sweat will be
Both for horses and men! How many funerals
Will you cause for your race! Pallas prepares her shield,
    Helmet, chariot, and her wrath!

In vain: trusting in vain Venus' protection, shall
You comb out your fair locks; with your unwarlike lyre
Shall you sing forth your songs pleasing to women's ears;
    In vain trusting the marriage bed,

You will seek to escape barbs of the Cretan darts,
Heavy spears, din of war, Ajax's swift pursuit,
Yet alas! and too late—much too late! you will soil
    Those adulterous locks with dust.

Look behind you, and see! There is Laertes' son
And the doom of your race! Nestor of Pylos, too!
Close upon you they press, Teucer of Salamis,
    There is Sthenelus skilled in war;

If the task is to curb horses, he'll not be a
Lazy charioteer. See Meriones! Look!
Dread Tydides is there, raging to seek you out,
    He, a better man than his sire,

He whom soon you will flee, as a weak stag with head
High and breathing the wind, heedless of grass, flees a
Wolf seen over the vale; you did not promise such
    Things as these to your light of love!

Though Achilles' hot wrath long shall defer the doom
Of the women of Troy, Ilium's fateful day;
After predestined years then shall you see the Greek
    Torches burning the homes of Troy!"[4]

---

[1] Paris, carrying Helen of Sparta off to Troy.

[2] Nereus, the wise old man of the sea, predicts the Trojan War and the doom of Troy.

[3] Thus the Greeks: "An ox or an ass that may happen to pass,/A cry or a word by chance overheard. If you deem it an omen you call it a bird." (Aristophanes, *The Birds*, 719 sqq. Translation by J. Hookham Frere, London, New York, 1909.)

[4] Metre: Third Asclepiadean.

O lovely daughter,[1] lovelier than your mother,
Put to my vile iambics what end you will,
    Whether by fire you please to burn them,
        Or toss them out in the Adriatic.

Not Dindymene,[2] nor does Apollo shake
The souls of priests who serve in the sacred shrine,
    Nor Bacchus, nor the Corybantes[3]
        Clashing sharp cymbal on cymbal, shake us

So much as wrath, which neither a Noric[4] blade,
Shipwrecking sea, the blaze of a raging fire,
    Nor Jupiter himself from heaven
        Falling with terrible tumult hinders.

For it is said Prometheus, forced to add
To primal clay bits cut off from everywhere,
    Imposed thereon the savage, maddened
        Strength of a lion to our vexation.

Now wrath laid low Thyestes[5] with grievous hurt,
And in our greatest cities stood forth for doom
    As primal cause why they have perished
        Utterly, cause why a host, exulting,

Drove hostile plowshares over their fallen walls.
Restrain your temper! Passion aroused me, too,
    When I was young, and into swiftly
        Moving iambics it sent me raging!

But now I seek to change cruel words to kind,
Provided once again you will be my friend,
So—with my slanders all recanted,
    Sweetly restore me to your affection![6]

[1] Shorey (*Horace—Odes and Epodes,* 192) says of this ode: "It is variously inscribed to Tyndaris, Gratidia, or Canidia. The mock-heroic tone is too playful for a serious recantation of the attack on the witch Canidia in Epodes 5 and 17; and the whole may be a mere exercise in verse writing."

[2] The great mother of the gods, Cybele, who symbolized the fruitfulness of nature.

[3] Priests of Cybele.

[4] Noricum, a country between the Danube and the Alps, was famous for its iron.

[5] The banquet of Thyestes, whose own sons were served up to him by his brother Atreus, was typical of the horrors of Greek tragedy.

[6] Metre: Alcaic Strophe.

Fleet Faunus[1] often leaves his Lycaean hill
To visit fair Lucretilis[2] now and then;
    And from my she-goats wards off fiery
        Heat, and protects them from rainy windstorms.

Unharmed, they seek wild strawberries lying hid
Among the shrubs and thyme in the sheltered grove;
    A fetid spouse's mates, they wander;
        Nor do their kids fear the young, green serpents,

Nor wolves beloved by Mars, when from Faunus' pipe,
His joyous pipe, O Tyndaris,[3] echo sounds
    From valleys and the smooth-worn rocks of
        Ustica's hillside so gently sloping.

The gods protect me; dear to their hearts my Muse,
My reverence. For you, from a kindly horn
    Shall flow in generous abundance
        All the rewards of our rural bounty.

Here in this vale secluded, you will escape
The Dog Star's heat; you'll sing with your Teian[4] lute
    About Penelope and dazzling
        Circe, both struggling with love for one man.

Here will you quaff the innocent Lesbian wine
Beneath the shade; here neither will Bacchus wage
    His wars with Mars, nor need you here be
        Anxious because of that jealous Cyrus,

Dread lest his hand, incontinent, snatch away
The leafy crown that clings to your pretty hair;
   And, though no match for him, you need not
      Fear lest he tear at your guiltless garment.[5]

---

[1] Faunus was the god of agriculture and shepherds; later identified with Pan.
[2] A mountain above Horace's Sabine farm.
[3] A fictitious name.
[4] The reference is to Anacreon, a lyric poet of Teos.
[5] Metre: Alcaic Strophe.

Plant, O Varus,[1] no tree in Tibur's soil, neither around the walls
Guarding Catilus'[2] town ere you first plant sacred and fruitful vines.
For to those who abstain, God has set out all things most difficult,
Nor shall gnawing despairs scatter and flee in any other way.
After wine who laments hardships of war, prattles of being poor?
Who would not rather speak, Bacchus, of you, and, lovely Venus, you?
And yet, who to excess uses the gifts Liber,[3] the mild, has giv'n
Is a warning, as when Centaurs[4] fought out with the Lapitheans
The fierce quarrels they had over their wine; Evius stern and harsh
Toward the Sithonians who, in their greed, separate right from wrong
By the fine line alone of their desires. I shall not rouse you thus,
O bright Bassareus,[5] flouting your will, nor shall I snatch to light
Symbols hidden beneath various leaves. Hush the harsh timbrel's noise,
Berecynthian[6] horns, for in their train follows a blind self-love;
And vainglory comes next, preening too much, tossing an empty head;
And faith spilling its trusts, pouring them out clearer than shining glass.[7]

[1] Varus is probably the Quintilius of I, 24.
[2] A brother of Tiburtus, with whom he built Tibur.
[3] An old Italian god of fructification and planting, sometimes identified with
Bacchus, the god of wine and poets.
[4] The strife arose out of the assault of the drunken Centaurs on the bride
Hippodamia at the wedding of Pirithoüs, king of the Lapithae.
[5] A title of Bacchus.
[6] The Berecynthian horn belonged to the worship of Cybele, but was transferred to that of Bacchus also.
[7] Metre: Fifth Asclepiadean.

Cruel mother of tender loves,[1]
She and Semele's[2] son, passion's unruly surge,
    These command me to let my soul
Now return to amours which I had thought were done.
    Burned by Glycera's[3] charm am I,
Shining purer than shines Parian marble's hue;
    Burned am I by her coquetry
And her dazzling smooth face, more than my eyes can stand.
    Venus now has forsaken her
Cyprus,[4] rushing toward me, neither will she permit
    Me to sing of the Scythians
Or the bold Parthians mounted on wheeling steeds;
    Nor do such things affect me now.
Here place turf for me, boys; here place me sacred boughs,
    Incense, bowl of a two-year wine:
With a sacrifice made, she will become more kind.[5]

[1] Venus.

[2] Semele; a daughter of Cadmus and mother of Bacchus by Jupiter.

[3] A woman's name.

[4] Cyprus; an island in the Mediterranean, celebrated for the worship of Venus. Venus will not allow Horace to praise the ambitions and triumph of Rome in the East.

[5] Metre: Second Asclepiadean.

You will drink cheap Sabine from modest goblets,
Juice I stored myself in a Grecian wine jar,
Sealed that day when plaudits to you were given
    There in the theater;

O dear knight Maecenas, when joyous echoes[1]
Rang across the Vatican Hill, at once your
Parents' river's banks would return them to you,
    Bearing our praises.

Caecuban[2] and wines from Calenian presses,
Finer wines you'll drink there; but here, the hills of
Formia do not flavor my cups, nor do
    Vines[3] of Falernus.[4]

---

[1] The plaudits of the people welcoming Maecenas back to Pompey's theater in the Campus Martius after an illness.

[2] Caecuban and Formian (from southern Latium) and Calenian and Falernian (from Campania) were all fine wines.

[3] Falernus: an Italian region famous for its wines.

[4] Metre: Sapphic Strophe.

Sing of Diana, sing! delicate maidens all,
Sing, O youths, of the god unshorn, the Cynthian;[1]
    Sing of Latona![2] Sing her
      Loved most deeply by Jove on high!

Sing, you maidens, of her happy by flowing streams,
Under leaves of the woods chilly on Algidus,[3]
    Or on black Erymanthus[4]
      Or on Cragus'[5] green-wooded slopes;

Praise now, all you young men, Tempe, Apollo's home,
Praise the place of his birth, Delos that beauteous isle,
    And his shoulder adorned with
      Quiver and with his brother's lyre.

He then, moved by your prayers, far from our populace
Will drive off tearful war, famine, and wretched plague
    To the Persians and Britons,
      Under Caesar's great leadership.[6]

[1] Apollo was so called, from Mt. Cynthus in Delos where he and Diana were born.
[2] Mother of Apollo and Diana.
[3] A high-wooded and snow-capped mountain near Rome, a haunt of Diana.
[4] A mountain in Arcadia.
[5] A promontory in Lycia.
[6] Metre: Fourth Asclepiadean.

Upright, whole of heart, undefiled by sin, man
Needs no Moorish javelin, neither bow, nor
Yet a quiver heavy with poisoned arrows—
    None of these, Fuscus[1]—

Whether lies his path through the scorching Syrtis,[2]
Or through hostile Caucasus[3] be his journey,
Even though it lead to those lands where flows the
    Fabled Hydaspes.[4]

For indeed I strolled to the farthest reach of
Sabine woodlands, Lalage's[5] praises singing,
Free of care; and sudden, a wolf fled from me,
    Though I was unarmed;

Such a beast as neither warlike Apulia[6]
Nourishes in forests of oak trees spreading,
Nor the land of Juba[7] has ever borne, that
    Dry nurse of lions.

Place me then in fields that are ever barren,
Where no tree is freshened by summer breezes,
Such a part of earth as the fog and sullen
    Jupiter presses;

Place me 'neath the course of the sun close beating,
Land denied for homes to the race of mankind;
Still I'll love the laughing, the sweet, the gentle
    Lalage's prattle.[8]

1 A man's name, probably a friend of Horace.

2 The reference is to the hot sands of the desert in the neighborhood of the Syrtes (two gulfs on the north coast of Africa).

3 A chain of rough mountains, inhabited by wild tribes, in Asia between the Black and Caspian seas.

4 A river of India.

5 The name of a young girl.

6 Horace's native province in southwestern Italy.

7 The land of Juba was Mauretania, a country of Africa on the coast of the Mediterranean.

8 Metre: Sapphic Strophe.

Chloe, shy as a fawn seeking her nervous dam
Up trackless mountain height, so do you flee from me;
    Empty fear of the soft breeze
        Holds her, frightened of woodland shade.

When the coming of spring rustles the moving leaves,
When the green lizards peer out through the bramble bush,
    Startled, foolishly frightened
        She stands trembling in heart and knees.

Yet no tiger am I, African lion fierce,
Nor do I follow you, thinking to do you harm:
    Leave your mother, my dear child,
        You are ripe for a man's love now.[1]

[1] Metre: Fourth Asclepiadean.

I, 24

Ah, what shame could there be, grieving for one so dear?
Or what end to this grief? You, whom the Father gave
Liquid voice and a lyre; you, O Melpomene[1]
    Teach us now to sing mourning songs!

So—perpetual sleep weighs down Quintilius![2]
When and where shall we find any to equal him?
Naked Truth, stainless Faith, sister of Justice—oh,
    Where shall Modesty find his peer?

Mourned by many good men, now he is perished; and
Is lamented by none, none, Vergil, more than you.
You petition the gods vainly, alas! for him,
    Not entrusted to them for this.

What? If you, with more charm than Thracian Orpheus,
Should attune the sweet lyre heard by the listening trees,
Would the blood then return into those hollow wraiths,
    Whom, with dreadful caduceus,

Cruel Mercury forced into his sable flock,
And, in spite of all prayers, will not unlock the Fates?
Hard it is: but those things which it is wrong to change
    Patience lightens for us to bear.[3]

[1] The Muse of tragedy.
[2] This is probably the (Quintilius) Varus of Book I, Ode 18.
[3] Metre: Third Asclepiadean.

53

Rarely now against your closed panes do young men
Toss the stones they once used to throw so boldly,
Neither do they rob you of sleep, the door clings
    Fast to the threshold,

Which before swung easily on its hinges.
Less and less already you hear the whisper:
"Long nights through, I'm perishing for you, Lydia,[1]
    And are you sleeping?"

Now in turn despised, in a lonely alley,
You, grown old, shall weep for your haughty lovers—
Weep, as underneath a new moon, the Thracian[2]
    Wind howls more loudly;

When an eager lust and a blazing passion
(As is wont to madden the dams of horses)
Rages 'round your liver, inflamed and burning,
    Not without sighs that

Joyous youth delights in fresh-growing ivy
Rather, and in leaves of the dusky myrtle;
Withered fronds he gives to the river Hebrus,
    Crony of winter.[3]

[1] An aging courtesan.
[2] That is, the northeast wind.
[3] Metre: Sapphic Strophe.

I, 26

The Muse's friend, I cast all my grief and care
To wanton winds to bear to the Cretan Sea;
    What king of icy shores beneath the
        Bear[1] may be feared is not my concern; or

What may terrify Tiridates[2] I
Care not. O sweet Pimplea,[3] you who delight
    In untouched springs, weave sunny flowers,
        Weave now a garland of song for Lamia.[4]

Without you, my own gifts are of no avail:
Immortalize him, you and your sisters, now
    With new-struck chords—as is befitting!—
        Using the ivory quill[5] of Lesbos.[6]

[1] The double constellation of the Great and Little Bear.

[2] King of Parthia in place of Phrahates, expelled for tyranny. Phrahates sought aid of the Scythians to recover his throne, and Tiridates fled to Augustus in Syria (30 B.C.).

[3] Reference is to the Muse of Pimplea, a place and fountain in Pieria near Mt. Olympus, sacred to the Muses.

[4] L. Aelius Lamia, a friend of Horace, and probably the consul of 2 A.D.

[5] That is, in a lyric in the manner of the Lesbian school.

[6] Metre: Alcaic Strophe.

In goblets meant for gladness, the Thracians[1] fight,
In drink they battle; banish that custom here,
    Away with it; defend our modest
        Bacchus from barbarous, blood-stained brawling.

How great a distance separates Persian dirk
From lights and wine—prodigious how far apart!
    Then hush this godless clamor, comrades,
        Rest on your elbows, at ease reclining.

Of strong Falernian wine do you wish me, too,
To take my share? Megilla's[2] young brother then!—let
    Him tell whose wound has made him happy,
        Say by whose arrow he now is dying!

He hesitates? I'll drink on no other terms!
Whichever Venus tames you, my boy, she burns
    Your heart with flames you need not blush for—
        Always you sin with a freeborn beauty!

So come and whisper now in my prudent ears
Whate'er you have to say . . . . Ah, poor wretched boy!
    In what Charybdis[3] are you struggling,
        You who are worthy of better burning!

What witch, or what magician of Thessaly[4]
With brewed enchantments, what god can set you free?
    Why, scarce could Pegasus release you,
        Snared in that threefold Chimaera's[5] clutches![6]

1 Thrace was a Roman province, now in Bulgaria, Greece, and Turkey.
2 Probably a girl's name.
3 A dangerous whirlpool between Italy and Sicily.
4 Thessaly was the land of brewed enchantments.
5 A fabulous monster in Lycia, which vomited forth fire, slain by Bellerophon.
6 Metre: Alcaic Strophe.

You who have measured the earth and the sea and the sands lacking number,
    Small gifts of dust now confine you, Archytas,[1]
Only the gift of a handful of soil near the shore of Matinum;
    Nor does it profit that you have attempted
Airy abodes, and that you in your thinking encompassed the rounded
    Dome of the heavens, since you must needs perish!
Tantalus died, who was guest of the gods, and Tithonus borne skyward,
    Minos, admitted to secrets of Jove; and
Tartarus holds, too, the offspring of Panthoüs sent for a second
    Time down to Orcus, although he had proved a
Witness to Trojan times, taking the shield from the wall of the temple,
    And had conceded his skin and his sinews
Unto black death, nothing more had he yielded; you would not consider
    Him a mean champion of truth and of nature—
Not in your judgment! But one and the same night is waiting for all, and
    Sometime the pathway of death must be trodden.
Still do the Furies present some with Mars' grim, spectacular gaming;
    Deadly the sea is, and greedy for sailors;
Corpses are crowded together and mingled, the young and the aged,
    No head escapes from the savage Proserpina:
Me also Notus, the South Wind, swift comrade of setting Orion,
    Drowned in Illyrian waves. But you, sailor,
Are not so niggardly as to refuse just a handful of wind-blown
    Sand to these bones, to this head still unburied:
Whate'er the threat which the East Wind has made to Hesperian billows,
    Let the Venusian forests be punished,
So you be safe; and may many rewards from all sides then flow toward you
    Whenever possible, may they flow down from
Jove, the impartial, and Neptune, protector of sacred Tarentum.

Would you then count it a light thing to do wrong,
Wrong which may afterward injure your innocent sons? And, perchance, stern
    Justice and punishment wait for you, also:
Though all my prayers go unanswered, I'll not be forsaken or slighted,
    Nor shall atonement for sinning absolve you.
Although you hasten, delay will not keep you long; soon you can sail on
    After three handfuls of dust have been scattered.[2]

---

[1] This ode, in the beautiful metre of the Alcmanian Strophe, is apparently the dramatic monologue of the ghost of one who has been shipwrecked near the tomb of the philosopher Archytas on the shore near Venusia. The ghost is represented as imploring with mingled entreaties and imprecations a passing sailor to give it the formal rites of burial—three handfuls of earth. Archytas of Tarentum was a Pythagorean philosopher and mathematician, and a contemporary of Plato.

[2] Metre: Alcmanian Strophe.

O Iccius,[1] to Araby's happy wealth
Do you look now? And do you prepare fierce war
    For those Sabaean[2] kings unconquered,
        Chains for the terrible Persian forging?

What strange, what savage, barbarous maiden then,
Her lover slain, will serve and attend your wants;
    What royal page with locks anointed
        Stand as your cupbearer close beside you,

Who once was taught the Serican arrow's aim
From father's bowstring? Who will deny that streams
    Reversed can glide up steepest mountains,
        Drawing the flow of the Tiber backward,

When you exchange (who promised us better things!)
The books you bought of noble Panaetius,
    Or leave the school of Socrates, to
        Shine in a corselet of Spanish armor?[3]

---

[1] Iccius, the scholar, is leaving for war. The expedition referred to is the unsuccessful campaign of Aelius Gallus in the year 25 B.C. In bantering tone, Horace expects Iccius to subdue the entire Orient.
[2] Saba: Sheba.
[3] Metre: Alcaic Strophe.

I, 30

Venus, queen of Cnidus,[1] O queen of Paphos,[2]
Spurn your chosen Cyprus, and with much incense
Come then, come, to Glycera's[3] graceful temple;[4]
    Sweetly she calls you.

Ardent Cupid, nymphs with their loosened girdles
Hasten after you and attend your coming,
Joys of youth that charm not without your presence,
    Mercury also.[5]

[1] Cnidus: a Dorian town in Caria; Venus was its tutelary divinity.
[2] Paphos: in Cyprus, also closely connected with the cult of Venus.
[3] A woman's name.
[4] Shorey (*Horace—Odes and Epodes*, 224) says: "It is probably Glycera's whole house that is spoken of as a temple of Venus. Others think that the reference is to a little shrine which Glycera had set up in her house."
[5] Metre: Sapphic Strophe.

What does the bard desire at Apollo's shrine?[1]
What does he pray for, as from the bowl he pours
    So freely forth the pure, new wine? Not
        Fruitful Sardinia's[2] fields so fertile,

Not summery Calabria's[3] pleasant herds,
Not gold nor India's ivory does he ask,
    Nor rustic farms where nibbles still the
        Deep-flowing Liris[4] with quiet water.

Let those to whom good Fortune gave vines, then prune
Them with Calenian[5] knife; let the wealthy man,
    The merchant, drain from golden goblets
        Wines which he purchased with wares from Syria;

Dear to the gods, since three or four times a year
He goes to the Atlantic and back again
    In safety. Me, the olives nourish,
        My food is chicory and light mallows.

Let me enjoy then, healthful and sound of mind,
I pray, Latoe![6] things I already have;
    And let my old age not be blemished,
        Neither, I pray, let me spend it songless.[7]

[1] This ode is the poet's prayer on the dedication of the temple on the Palatine Hill to Actian Apollo, 28 B.C.
[2] Sardinia, with Sicily and Africa, the granary of Rome.
[3] Calabria, in southern Italy, had excellent pasture lands.
[4] The Liris, a river between Latium and Campania.
[5] Cales, in Campania, was a center of the wine-growing industry.
[6] Latoe: son of Latona, i.e., Apollo.
[7] Metre: Alcaic Strophe.

We are asked for song. If the songs we sang in
Idle hour, 'neath shade and in playful vein, now
Live and will live—come, let us sing a Latin[1]
    Strain, O my lyre, first

Tuned by him of Lesbos, that citizen[2] who,
Fierce in warfare, still in the midst of battle,
Or if he had moored on the wave-washed shore his
    Tempest-tossed vessel,

Used to sing of Liber, the Muses, Venus
And the boy who always is clinging to her,
Sang the praise of Lycus, so beautiful with
    Black eyes and black hair.

Tortoise shell[3] of Phoebus,[4] his pride and glory,
Welcome at the feasts of almighty Jove, O
Sweet relief from toil, when I duly call you,
    Hark to my pleading![5]

---

[1] Latin: emphatic, for it was with Greek poetry that the lyre was associated chiefly. Lyric verse was considered trifling by the Romans; yet Horace proudly considers himself both an imitator and a rival of the Greeks.

[2] The reference is to Alcaeus, the Greek poet whom Horace greatly admired, and who was emphatically a patriot and a political poet.

[3] The arched shape of the tortoise shell was adapted to use in stringing the lyre.

[4] Phoebus: a poetic appellation of Apollo, the god of music and poetry.

[5] Metre: Sapphic Strophe.

Albius,[1] do not grieve too much, remembering
Cruel-sweet Glycera, neither sing mournful songs
Sadly questioning why, why she broke faith, and a
    Younger lover outshines you now.

On Lycoris'[2] low brow, love marks its burning brand
As for Cyrus she sighs; Cyrus, in turn, looks toward
Sharp-tongued Pholoe; but sooner will delicate
    Deer be paired with Apulian wolves

Than will Pholoe stoop to a base libertine.
This to Venus seems fit, she who is pleased to join
Unmatched natures and souls under a yoke of bronze,
    And enjoys such a savage jest.[3]

As for me: once when love, better love, sought me out,
Myrtale, a freed slave, held me with pleasing chains;
She was stormier far than Adriatic waves
    On Calabria's curving gulfs.[4]

[1] Albius Tibullus, the elegiac poet; yet there is no Glycera mentioned in his extant elegies, the sentimentality of which might have seemed excessive to Horace.
[2] Lycoris, like Cyrus and Pholoë, is a fictitious name.
[3] This poem is simply a light touching on the theme that "Love mocks us all."
[4] Metre: Third Asclepiadean.

A scant, infrequent worshipper of the gods,[1]
Schooled in a mad philosophy late I strayed,
    But now I am compelled to turn my
        Sails and retrace my forsaken courses.

For truly did Diespiter,[2] lord of light,
Who ofttimes cleaves the clouds with his flashing fire,
    Through skies serene, unclouded, drive his
        Thundering steeds and his wheeling chariot,

Whereby the sluggish earth and the wand'ring streams,
Whereby the Styx and Taenarus,[3] mouth of hell,
    And Atlas[4] at the world's far end is
        Shaken. For God has the power of changing

The low to high, can humble the famous man,
Bring forth the hidden; Fortune,[5] the spoiler, oft
    Has snatched away a crown with crackling
        Rustle of wings, and enjoyed the doing![6]

---

[1] A clap of thunder from a cloudless sky has apparently shaken Horace from his youthful belief that the gods "lie beside their nectar careless of mankind."

[2] Diespiter: an archaic word for Jupiter as the lord of light and god of day.

[3] The Styx was one of the rivers of the infernal regions. Taenarus was a rift in the rocks at Taenarum, a promontory on the south coast of the Peloponnesus, and was deemed the mouth of hell.

[4] Atlas, the mountain range in northwest Africa, was regarded as the western limit of the world.

[5] Fortune was considered to be a winged goddess.

[6] Metre: Alcaic Strophe.

O goddess,[1] you who rule your loved Antium,[2]
O queen with power to lift from the lowest rank
    Man's mortal clay, you who have power to
        Change to disaster our splendid triumphs,

With anxious prayer the farmer beseeches you,
And whosoever dares in Bithynian[3] bark
    To furrow the Carpathian Sea, O
        Mistress of waters, he, too, entreats you;

Wild Dacians fear you, wandering Scythians,
All towns and tribes and Latium, fierce and bold,
    The mothers of barbarian kings, and
        Purple-clad tyrants all dread and fear you,

Lest with affronting foot you should overthrow
The standing column, or lest the crowding throng
    Incite the mob "To arms! To arms!" and
        Rouse them to shatter the strength of empire.

Before you always savage Necessity
Proceeds with spikes and wedge in her brazen hand,
    The dreaded hook is never lacking,
        Nor is the hot, molten lead for pouring.

But Hope abides with you, and rare Constancy
In robe of white, nor does she refuse herself
    As comrade when, with change of garment,
        You, like a foeman, leave homes once mighty.

The fickle crowd, the false-swearing courtesan,
They all move back, these friends, when our casks are drained
    Of wine, and only dregs are left; too
        Crafty are they to share our misfortunes.

Our Caesar's path to Britain[4] may you protect;
To earth's far ends, to ultimate lands he goes;
    Protect our swarms of youths, let them be
        Feared in the East and the Indian Ocean.

Alas, for shame, these wounds and these brothers' wars!
From what have we refrained, this our hardened age?
    What crime is left untried? From what, through
        Fear of the gods, has our youth held back or

Restrained its hand? What shrines has it ever spared?
Oh, that you might reforge now our blunted swords
    Anew against the Arabs and the
        Scythians east of the Caspian waters![5]

[1] This is the famous Ode to Fortune.

[2] The capital of the Volsci, on the coast of Latium, now Anzio. At the old oracle and temple of Fortune there, two images were consulted by lots and were supposed to give responses by their movements.

[3] Bithynia, on the south coast of the Black Sea, produced fine timber for ship-building.

[4] August contemplated an expedition to Britain in 27 B.C., but was detained in Gaul. The Arabian campaign of Aelius Gallus was in preparation in 26 B.C., the probable date of this ode.

[5] Metre: Alcaic Strophe.

Both with incense and with the lyre,
    Bull-calf's blood as their due, pleasant it is to win
Grace from Numida's[1] guardian gods,
    His who, now home again unharmed from farthest Spain,
Many kisses bestows on friends
    Dearly loved, but on none more than sweet Lamia
In remembrance of boyhood passed,
    Tender years which they spent 'neath the same teacher's rule,
Togas changed at the selfsame time.[2]
    So then let this fair day lack not its white chalk mark,
Bring forth wine jars unlimited,
    Bring no rest to the feet dancing in Salian mode,[3]
Nor let Damalis,[4] many-wined,
    Outdo Bassus at draughts, drinking in Thracian style;[5]
Let our feast lack no roses then,
    Neither parsley long-lived, nor the brief lily's bloom.
All on Damalis then will fix
    Fast their languishing eyes; yet she will not be torn
From her newly found paramour,
    Clinging closer to him than wanton ivy vine.[6]

---

[1] This ode is a welcome to Plotius Numida on his return from the west, probably from the Spanish campaign of Augustus in 27–25 B.C.

[2] The formal changing of the *toga praetexta* for the *toga virilis* took place at about the age of sixteen, and was the assumption of the garb of manhood.

[3] The Salii, or jumpers, were, so to speak, the dancing dervishes of Mars.

[4] Damalis: a frequent name of girls of her class. Bassus is unknown.

[5] The Thracian characteristically drained a cup at a gulp.

[6] Metre: Second Asclepiadean.

Now[1] is the time for drinking, now is the time
With foot set free to stamp on the ground, and now,
    Oh, now the time with Salian[2] feasts to
        Honor the couch of the gods, my comrades!

Before this moment, it had been sin to draw
The Caecuban[3] from ancestral vaults below,
    The while the maddened queen was planning
        Ruin for Rome and a grave for empire.

With her polluted crew of base, shameful men[4]
She planned; and she was frenzied enough to hope
    For anything, for she was then so
        Drunk with sweet fortune. But fury faded

When only one ship barely escaped the flames;[5]
Her mind, already crazed by Egyptian wine,
    Did Caesar drive to true fear as she
        Fled forth from Italy, and he followed

With urgent oars as hawk does the gentle doves,
Or hunter follows hare on the snowy fields
    Of Thessaly; pressed close that he might
        Put her in chains, this portentous monster.

But seeking for the means to a nobler death,
She did not fear the sword, as is woman's way,
    Nor tried by her swift fleet to find some
        Place of concealment on hidden coast lines.

She even dared to visit her fallen court
With tranquil brow, and bravely she dared lay hold
    Of scaly serpents, that she might drink
        Into her body their deadly venom.

Determined still more boldly on death, she grudged
The fierce Liburnian[6] galleys, and scorned to be
    A discrowned queen led forth in triumph—
        She was no humble or tame-souled woman![7]

[1] A song of triumph over the defeat of Antony and Cleopatra at the Battle of
Actium, 31 B.C. This ode was apparently written when the news of Cleopatra's
suicide reached Rome, possibly in the autumn of 30 B.C.
[2] That is, as magnificent as those of the Salii, priests of Mars, the luxury of
whose banquets was proverbial.
[3] Caecuban: a fine wine.
[4] The Eunuchs.
[5] The escape of barely one ship: it was the fleet of Antony that was thus destroyed. Cleopatra fled early during the engagement, and Antony followed her.
Horace pictures Caesar as then giving chase; as a matter of fact, however, he returned to Italy to quiet a mutiny of the veterans quartered at Samos, and entered
Egypt only in the following spring.
[6] The swift, light Liburnian galleys proved especially effective at the battle of
Actium.
[7] Metre: Alcaic Strophe.

I, 38

I hate Persian luxury,[1] boy, I hate it;[2]
Crowns of flowers on linden-bark strips annoy me;
Stop that eager running around to where a
    Late rose might linger.

So take care, add nothing to simple myrtle:
It's not unbecoming to you, a servant—
Nor to me as, under a trellised vine, I
    Tend to my drinking![3]

[1] Persian luxury would include unnecessary additions to the simple requirements of the wise Epicurean.
[2] This charming trifle is probably intended to relieve the severity of the several odes immediately preceding it.
[3] Metre: Sapphic Strophe.

BOOK II

*"Whosoever chooses the golden mean, that
Man is safe and free...."* — II, 10

Of civic turmoil, causes of war, mistakes,
From back to when Metullus was consul, of
　　Its blunders, turns, the sport of Fortune,
　　　　Fateful alliances of our leaders,

Of bloodstained arms—our blood and not yet atoned!—
You undertake a task full of peril now
　　To write of these; the while you tread on
　　　　Fires hidden under deceitful ashes.

Then let the Muse of tragedy grim and stern
Absent herself from theaters for a while;
　　With public facts set forth in order,
　　　　You will resume the Cecropian buskin.[1]

For you are famed defending the sad accused,
And counseling the Senate, my Pollio[2]
　　To whom the laurel brought eternal
　　　　Honors you earned in Dalmatian triumph.

Already now with threatening sound of horn
You deafen us, already the trumpets' blare,
　　Already armor fiercely shining
　　　　Frightens the horses, the horsemen's faces.

I seem to hear already of mighty chiefs
All stained with not inglorious dust, and see
　　The whole of earth subdued and conquered—
　　　　All but the staunch, stubborn soul of Cato.[3]

For Juno and the gods who, though friendlier
To Africa, unable to aid withdrew,
    Have offered up the victors' grandsons
        Now to the shades of the slain Jugurtha.[4]

What field, more fertile thus by our Latin blood,
Does not, with graves, to impious battles fought
    Bear witness, and has not the sound of
        Italy's downfall been heard in Persia?

What flood or river is there which does not know
Our mournful warfare? Where an Italian sea
    Which slaughter's gore has not discolored?
        Where is the shore which is free of bloodstains?

Lay not aside your jests, my audacious Muse,
To undertake the task of a Cean[5] dirge;
    With me in Dionean[6] grotto,
        Seek still such strains with your lighter[7] plectrum.[8]

[1] Cecrops was the founder of Athens, the home of tragedy. The buskin was the boot worn by the tragic actor. It had a high sole to give the tragedian a more imposing appearance.

[2] C. Asinius Pollio had been a friend of Cicero in his youth and a member of the circle of Calvus and Catullus. He had studied at Athens a few years before Horace's stay there, and had fought under Caesar at Pharsalus. After his consulate (40 B.C.) he was sent against the Parthini, a Dalmatian tribe, by Antony, and celebrated a triumph over them (39 B.C.). From the spoils of this campaign, he established the first public library at Rome. His history of the civil wars in seventeen books is mentioned by Tacitus, Suetonius, and others.

[3] M. Porcius Cato, the younger, the enemy of Caesar, who committed suicide after the battle of Pharsalia, at Utica. He was the idol of Stoics and declaimers.

[4] Jugurtha, the nephew and successor of Micipsa, king of Numidia, conquered by Marius in the war with the Romans. Juno, in the legend, was the opponent of Aeneas and the patron of Carthage, and so of Africa against Italy.

[5] Simonides of Ceos, who wrote the epitaphs on the heroes of Thermopylae and Salamis, was noted for his pathos.

[6] Dione was the mother of Venus, but here the name is used for Venus.

[7] The plectrum was a little stick with which the player struck the chords of a stringed instrument. It is used here to mean lyric poetry.

[8] Metre: Alcaic Strophe.

Silver has no brightness concealed in avid
Earth, Crispus Sallustius,[1] you who scorn the
Wealth of beaten silver unless it shines by
    Well-tempered usage.

Long shall Proculeius[2] then live, well-known for
His paternal spirit shown toward his brothers:
Lifting him aloft on unflagging wing, his
    Fame shall outlive him.

Wider shall you reign by subduing greedy
Pride than joining Libya to distant Gades,[3]
And by having both those Phoenician countries
    Serve but one master.

Dropsy dire grows greater by self-indulgence,
Thirst assuages not till the cause of sickness
Shall have fled the veins, and the sluggish water
    Leaves the pale body.

Rightful reason, differing from the rabble,
Parts Phrahates[4] (back on the throne of Cyrus)
From those counted blest, and instructs the people
    Not to use false terms;

Bringing him alone a protected kingdom,
Safe and sure his crown, his own lasting laurel,
Who beholds with calm eye and no glance backward
    Great heaps of treasure.[5]

---

[1] Crispus Sallustius was the grandnephew and adopted son of the great historian, and was the owner of rich copper mines.

[2] C. Proculeius, the brother of Maecenas' wife Terentia and of L. Licinius Murena, shared his estate with his brothers, who lost their property in the civil wars.

[3] Libya in Africa and Gades (the modern Cadiz) in Spain.

[4] Phrahates, expelled from Parthia for tyranny, had recovered his throne. The meaning here is that the true king is not he who sits on the throne of Cyrus, but the man who governs himself well.

[5] Metre: Sapphic Strophe.

II, 3

Remember to preserve an unruffled mind,
Though hard and steep your path; in prosperity
    Likewise no overweening gladness,
        Dellius,[1] since you are doomed to perish,

What though you lived in sadness through all your years,
What though in some far meadow you leaned at ease
    And through the festal days took pleasure
        There with the choicest Falernian vintage.

Why do the silver poplar and mighty pine
Delight to join their boughs into welcome shade?
    Why does the fleeing water strive to
        Hurry along in its winding channel?

Here bid them bring the wines and the fragrant oils,
The too-brief blossomings of the lovely rose,
    While youth and fortune and the sable
        Thread of the Three Sisters[2] still permit it.

For you will leave the woodlands which once you bought,
Your home, your villa the tawny Tiber laves,
    Yes, you will leave; your heir will lord it
        Over the wealth you piled up so proudly.

It matters not a whit if you're rich or poor,
Of lowly birth or Inachus'[3] ancient line,
    You linger 'neath the light of heaven,
        Victim of Orcus[4] who knows no pity.

We all are driven, all, to the selfsame place,
And later . . . sooner . . . out of the shaken urn[5]
Our lot will leap; on Charon's[6] bark then
We shall be set toward eternal exile![7]

[1] Quintus Dellius, the boon companion of Antony, was (so Shorey, in his *Horace—Odes and Epodes*, page 254, tells us) wittily nicknamed by Messalla *"desultor bellorum civilium,"* the *desultor* being the circus rider who leaps from horse to horse. His last change of front was his desertion of Antony for Octavian through fear of Cleopatra. He stood high in the favor of Augustus, and was the author of memoirs of the Parthian wars.

[2] The Greek fates: Clotho, who spun; Lachesis, who twisted; and Atropos, who severed the thread of life.

[3] Inachus: the first mythical king of Argos, here typical of ancient lineage.

[4] Orcus: the god of the infernal regions; Pluto; death.

[5] The urn in which the lots of all men are shaken by necessity. When a man's lot flies out, he must die.

[6] Charon: the ferryman of the river Styx, who carried the souls of the departed across to the lower world.

[7] Metre: Alcaic Strophe.

II, 4

Don't blush for your love of a serving maiden,
Xanthias of Phocis![1] Fair Briseïs, a
Snow-complexioned slave girl once long ago roused
    Haughty Achilles;

Once the grace of captive Tecmessa stirred her
Master, Ajax, Telamon's son; in midst of
Triumph, yet on fire for a captured virgin,
    Was Agamemnon,

When, beneath Thessalian attack, to weary
Greeks the foreign squadrons had fallen, and the
Death of Hector gave to their troops a Troy more
    Easily conquered.

You don't know: the parents of flax-haired Phyllis
May be rich and honor you as their son; no
Doubt she mourns lost royal estate and unkind
    Gods of her household!

Oh, don't think you chose from the vulgar rabble
Her so faithful, her so averse to gain! She
Could not have been born of a mother whom you
    Need feel ashamed of!

Arms and face and ankles so slim, heart-whole I
Praise: relax, dispel your suspicious fears of
One whose age the hurrying years have brought now
    Close onto forty![2]

[1] Xanthias of Phocis is as real or unreal as Gyges of Cnidus, or Calais, the son of Ornytus of Thurmium, or other names used by Horace for convenience. In this teasing ode he supplies heroic precedents for a gentleman who has fallen in love with a serving maid.
[2] Metre: Sapphic Strophe.

She[1] cannot bear the yoke on her bended neck
As yet, nor yet draw equally with her mate,
    Nor yet in venery sustain the
        Ponderous weight of a rushing bullock.

Your heifer's heart is busy with greening fields,
In cooling streams she eases the heavy heat,
    And now in marshy groves of willows
        Sports with a herd of desirous bull-calves.

Away with longing for the unripened grape,
Already changing autumn begins to streak
    For you the dullish, leaden, dark-blue
        Clusters of grapes with a purple beauty.

She soon will follow you; ruthless time speeds on,
And to her age will add all the years it cuts
    Away from yours; with wanton forehead
        Lalage soon will seek you as husband.

Coy Pholoe is not more beloved than she,
Nor Chloris with her shoulders as gleaming white
    As gleams the moon from cloudless sky at
        Night on the waves; nor is Cnidian Gyges,[2]

Whom if you were to mix with a throng of girls,
The difference so slight would deceive full well
The eyes of shrewdest strangers with his
Free-flowing locks and uncertain features.[3]

[1] Lalage is not yet ripe for love.
[2] Gyges of Cnidus is probably a fictitious name. Horace has in mind the story of Ulysses and Diomedes who cleverly detected Achilles hiding, disguised as a girl, among the daughters of Lycomedes.
[3] Metre: Alcaic Strophe.

O Septimius,[1] who would go with me to
Gades,[2] to Cantabrians[3] yet untaught to
Bear our yoke, where always the Moorish billow
    Surges, wild Syrtis:[4]

Would that Tibur, by a Greek farmer founded,
Might for my old age be the final haven,
Be my end at last, who am tired of sea and
    Highways and warfare.

Whence, if unkind Fates should prevent, then shall I
Seek Galaesus,[5] river so sweet to sheep, skin-
Covered, seek the countryside governed once by
    Spartan Phalanthus.[6]

There, of all the lands on the earth, that corner
Smiles at me, oh, there where the honey yields not
Even to Hymettus,[7] where olives rival
    Gray-green Venafrum's;[8]

There the spring which Jupiter grants is long, and
Winters mild; and Aulon,[9] beloved by fertile
Bacchus, toward Falernian grapes in clusters
    Looks with no envy.

You with me: that spot and those blissful summits
Both invite us; there to your poet-friend you'll
Pay your due by moistening with your tear his
    Still-glowing ashes.[10]

[1] A Septimius is recommended to the good offices of Tiberius (Horace, Epistles, I, 9), and the name recurs in a letter to Augustus.

[2] The pillars of Hercules, the proverbial limit of the known world; now Cadiz.

[3] A tribe in northwestern Spain.

[4] Sandbanks in the sea off the north coast of Africa.

[5] A river near Tarentum.

[6] The Spartan Phalanthus was said to have founded Tarentum.

[7] A mountain near Athens, famed for its honey.

[8] A city in northern Campania, noted for its olives.

[9] Probably a mountain slope suitable for vineyards.

[10] Metre: Sapphic Strophe.

O you who direst peril oft shared with me
When led by Brutus, captain of our campaign—
    Who has restored you as a Roman
        To your Italian gods and heavens,

Pompeius,[1] first of all my companions there,
With whom I broke the lingering day with wine,
    Yes, many times, when I had crowned my
        Gleaming locks shining with Syrian perfume?

With you I knew Philippi and took swift flight,
And, not with honor, left there my little shield,
    When strength was crushed, and threatening faces
        Struck with their chins on earth's dusty surface.

But, wrapped in cloud, swift Mercury bore me thence,
Me greatly frightened, right through the hostile ranks;
    While, sucking you again to war, a
        Wave bore you back to the surging channels.

Therefore to Jove now render the feast you owe,
And place your body, tired by long strife, beneath
    My bay tree, neither stint your drinking
        Freely from casks which are for your pleasure.

Then fill the polished cups with forgetful wine,
With Massic wine, from generous shells pour out
    The fragrant oils. And quickly, quickly,
        Who from fresh parsley will fix us chaplets?

Or else from myrtle? Whom now will Venus name
To judge the drinking bout? No more sanely than
 The Thracians shall I drink; it is so
  Maddening sweet to regain my comrade![2]

[1] Pompeius is unknown. Horace's account of his ignominious flight from Philippi can be taken with a chuckle and a grain of salt. The headlong rout, the loss
of his shield, and the downfall of the bold are indirect compliments to the valor
of Augustus.
[2] Metre: Alcaic Strophe.

If, for all your vows falsely sworn, Barina,[1]
Any punishment had been given; if, by
One black tooth or nail you were ever blemished,
    I might believe you!

But, whene'er you pledge to your empty vows your
Faithless head, you shine the more beautiful, and
Walk abroad, the common concern, the care of
    All our young manhood.

By your mother's ashes you swear—and falsely!
By the silent tokens of night, the whole sky,
By the gods exempt from chill death, and find it
    All to your profit!

Venus laughs herself at this, I repeat it;
All the guileless nymphs laugh, and cruel Cupid
Always sharp'ning up on his bloodstained whetstone
    Glittering arrows.

Add that all our youth keeps on growing for you,
Lovers new arise and become your servants,
Nor will old ones leave their light lady's dwelling,
    Though oft they threaten.

Mothers on account of their sons thus fear you,
Thrifty old men, too, and brides lately married,
Wretched, fearing lest your allure detain still
    Even their husbands![2]

---

1 A girl's name. This is simply a charming ode to a coquette.
2 Metre: Sapphic Strophe.

Not always from the clouds do the storms of rain
Pour down on shaggy fields, nor the rough'ning blasts
    Forever vex the Caspian waters;[1]
        Neither upon the Armenian coast lines,

O Valgius,[2] my friend, does the rigid ice
Stand all the months, nor under Aquilo's breath
    Do Gargan[3] oak trees strive, nor are the
        Wild ash trees widowed of all their leaflets.

You always dwell in dolorous manner still
On Mystes'[4] loss, nor yet do your passions die
    At Vesper's[5] rise, nor when she flees as
        Swiftly the sun courses up the heavens.

Yet that old man,[6] who three generations lived,
Wept not for sweet Antilochus[7] through them all;
    Not always did young Troilus'[8] parents
        Mourn for him, nor did his Trojan sisters.

So pray now, cease effeminate, weak complaints;
Let us instead sing Caesar Augustus and
    His new-won trophies; let us also
        Sing of the rugged, icebound Niphrates,[9]

And how the Medus[10] tumbles its lesser streams,
The river which we gained from those conquered tribes,
    And how the limited Geloni[11]
        Ride on their raids in their narrowed prairies.[12]

[1] The Caspian Sea was stormy.

[2] C. Valgius Rufus wrote elegies, medical and rhetorical works, and an epic, considered by Tibullus to be "Homeric."

[3] Garganus is an exposed, sea-girt promontory of Apulia.

[4] Mystes seems to be merely a name.

[5] The evening star.

[6] Nestor: son of Neleus and king of Pylos, famed for his wisdom and eloquence. He is said to have lived through three generations of men.

[7] A son of Nestor, who saved his father's life, and was slain by Hector before Troy.

[8] Troilus: son of Priam, slain by Achilles.

[9] Niphrates: a mountain in Armenia.

[10] The river Euphrates.

[11] A Sarmatian or Scythian tribe. Their limits had been narrowed by conquest.

[12] Metre: Alcaic Strophe.

Wiser shall you live, O Licinius,[1] by
Neither pressing always toward open water,
Nor, though heeding storms, hugging too close to the
    Uneven shore line.

Whosoever chooses the golden mean, that
Man is safe and free from a squalid roof, and
Soberly is free of a courtly mansion
    Apt to rouse envy.

Oftener by winds is the mighty pine tree
Shaken, lofty palaces fall with harder
Crash, and bolts of lightning more often strike the
    Tops of the mountains.

Still the heart, the well-prepared heart keeps hoping
Change of lot will come to the troubled, fears it
For the fortunate. Jupiter again brings
    Hideous winter,

And removes it. Not, if things now go badly,
Thus will they continue; Apollo sometimes
Wakes the silent Muse with his lute, not always
    Bends he his curved bow.

Spirited and brave in adverse conditions
Show yourself; and you will act wisely also,
When your sails are swollen by too strong wind, to
    Take in your canvas.[2]

[1] L. Licinius Murena, probably the son of the Murena of Cicero's *Pro Murena*, was adopted into the Terentian gens by Terentius Varro, and so became the adopted brother of Proculeius (II, 2) and of Terentia, the wife of Maecenas. Book III, Ode 19, is apparently written to celebrate his admission into the college of augurs. He appears in the consular calendar for the year 23 B.C. In the same year he was put to death for conspiring against Augustus—apparently after the publication of the first three books of the Odes. It seems unlikely that Horace would have included these poems in the Odes after Murena's death.

[2] Metre: Sapphic Strophe.

That which the warlike Spaniard and Scythian
Across the Adriatic may plot far off,
    Hirpinus Quintius,[1] forbear to
        Question; nor anxiously fret and worry

About the needs of age, whose demands are few.
Our smooth-cheeked youth and beauty flee fast behind,
    Our dry, gray locks repelling all those
        Frolicsome loves and that easy slumber.

Not always is the charm of spring blooms the same,
Nor does the blushing moon with but one face shine;
    Then why with those eternal schemings
        Must you fatigue your unequal spirit?

So why not drink beneath the tall plane or pine,
Reclining at our ease while it still is ours,
    Our hoary locks perfumed with roses,
        Oiled with Assyria's fragrant ointment?

For Evius[2] dispels our devouring cares.
Who'll cool our cups of burning Falernian?[3]
    Which slave boy will be quicker with the
        Water that runs in the flowing brooklet?

And who will lure the coy wench who lives alone?
Let Lyda come from home with her lyre inlaid
    With ivory; bid her make haste, her
        Hair in a knot like a Spartan maiden's.[4]

1 Unknown; probably a friend of Horace.
2 Evius: a surname of Bacchus, the god of wine.
3 A fine wine.
4 Metre: Alcaic Strophe.

You would surely not wish set to the lyre's sweet strains
The Numantian wars,[1] long and most tedious,
Nor stern Hannibal[2] sung, nor the Sicilian Sea
    Stained and reddened with Punic blood,

Nor the fierce Lapithae,[3] drunken Hylaeus,[4] nor
How by Hercules' hand giants of earth were felled,[5]
Whence such peril arose that ancient Saturn's house,
    Gleaming splendid, had rocked with fear:

You, Maecenas, will tell better in prose the tales
Of the wars Caesar fought; better that you should tell
How the threatening kings, chains 'round their necks, were led,
    Led in triumph along our streets.

Me, the Muse would have sing songs of Licymnia,[6]
Sing the lady sweet songs, sing her bright, shining eyes,
Her whose heart is so true, faithful indeed her heart
    To all loves who love her in turn;

Whom to join in the dance it does not ill become,
Nor to vie with a jest, neither to lend her arms
In the games with the maids shining in bright attire,
    Celebrating Diana's day.

Would you take in exchange wealth of Achaemenes[7]
Or the might of that rich Phrygian Mygdon[8] or
Fine Arabian homes full of their luxuries
    For one hair of Licymnia,

Though she turn but her neck now to your burning kiss,
Or if, playfully stern, she denies you the kiss
She enjoys to have snatched more than the one who begs,
    Sometimes snatching one first herself?[9]

[1] The Numantian wars lasted from 141–133 B.C., and were ended by Scipio Africanus Minor.

[2] Leader of the Carthaginians in the Second Punic War against Rome.

[3] A Thessalian people inhabiting the mountainous districts near Mounts Olympus and Pelion.

[4] A Centaur who offered violence to Atalanta.

[5] The oracle had declared that the gods could subdue the earthborn giants only with the aid of a mortal.

[6] The reference is probably to Terentia, the wife of Maecenas. A modern writer would hardly describe his friend's wife in this frank fashion; but Terentia's coquetry was common gossip.

[7] First king of Persia.

[8] A prince of Phrygia. Midas, whose touch turned all to gold, was king of Phrygia.

[9] Metre: Third Asclepiadean.

Some wretch it was, that luckless, ill-omened day,
Who planted you with impious hand, O tree,[1]
    And reared you to his shame to be the
        Bane of posterity and the village;

I could believe he strangled his aged sire;
In dead of night he spattered his inner rooms
    With blood and gore of trusting guests; oh,
        He was a dealer in Colchian[2] poisons,

And anywhere a horrible crime was hatched,
He planned it—he who stood you within my field,
    You sorry log, and destined you to
        Crash on the head of your guiltless master!

What each should shun as peril from hour to hour
Man never knows sufficient to guard against:
    The Punic sailor greatly dreads the
        Bosphorus, fearing no fate hid elsewhere;

The soldier fears the Parthian's arrowed flight,
The Parthian fears chains and Italian strength;
    And yet death's unexpected blight has
        Seized and will seize every race and nation.

We almost saw Proserpina's[3] gloomy realms,
Almost saw Aeacus[4] on the judgment seat,
    Abodes where dwell the blessed host, and
        Where with her Lesbian lyre sad Sappho[5]

Complains and sighs for girls of her native land;
And you, Alcaeus,[6] sound with your golden quill
    More loudly on your fuller strings the
        Hardships of sailing and war and exile.

The shades, amazed, in reverent silence stand
To hear these stories worthy of sacred awe,
    But shoulder close to drink the magic
        Tales of great battles and banished tyrants.

What wonder is it then that the spellbound beast[7]
At songs like these his hundred black ears drops down,
    That snakes entwined among the Furies'[8]
        Locks cease to writhe and are lulled to quiet?

Prometheus[9] and Tantalus[10] are beguiled
By this sweet sound to rest from their endless toil;
    Orion[11] cares no more for hunting,
        Lion and lynx rest in timid safety.[12]

[1] Humorous and exaggerated imprecations on a tree on Horace's Sabine farm that fell suddenly and barely missed the owner's head. Horace writes of his narrow escape from death.

[2] Medea, who came from Colchis, was known for her skill in concocting poisons.

[3] Wife of Pluto and queen of the underworld.

[4] A son of Jupiter by Europa, king of Aegina. On account of his justice he was made judge in the lower regions.

[5] Celebrated poetess, born at Mytilene in Lesbos, who, on account of her hopeless love for Phaon, threw herself from the Leucadian Rock into the sea.

[6] Alcaeus: lyric poet of Mytilene, the inventor of Alcaic verse.

[7] Cerberus has three heads generally, fifty in Hesiod, and one hundred in Pindar. He guarded the entrance to the lower world.

[8] The three goddesses of vengeance.

[9] Prometheus, who stole fire from heaven, is here represented by Horace as detained in Tartarus, contrary to all other versions of the myth.

[10] A king of Phrygia, admitted by Jupiter to the feasts of the gods; but he disclosed their secrets, and was sent as punishment to the lower regions.

[11] A celebrated hunter; the constellation into which Orion was changed.

[12] Metre: Alcaic Strophe.

Alas, the years glide, Postumus, Postumus,[1]
The fleeing years; no piety shall delay
    The wrinkles and relentless aging,
        Neither the menace of death's insistence;

Not with three hundred bulls offered every day,
Could you, friend, placate Pluto the tearless one,
    Who holds three-bodied Geryon[2] and
        Tityos,[3] too, with that gloomy river

Which must indeed be voyaged by all of us
Who feed upon earth's bountiful gifts; though we
    Be lords of earth or needy farmers,
        Still must that river be crossed by all men.

In vain from bloodstained Mars shall we hold aloof,
And from deep-sounding Adria's broken waves,
    In vain through autumns shall we fear the
        Harm to our bodies from scorching south winds:

For black Cocytus,[4] wand'ring with sluggish flow,
We still must visit, Danaüs' wicked race,[5]
    Must still see Sisyphus,[6] the son of
        Aeolus, doomed to eternal labor.

Lands must be left, and home, and your pleasant wife;
Nor of these trees you cultivate with such care,
    Except alone the hated cypress,
        Shall any follow their short-lived master.

Your heir, more worthy, then shall consume your wine,
Your Caecuban[7] locked up with a hundred keys,
    And stain your floor with noble vintage,
        Finer than that at the high-priests' banquets.[8]

1 Postumus is unknown; perhaps merely typical.
2 A giant with three bodies, slain by Hercules.
3 Tityos, who insulted Latona, was slain by her children, Apollo and Diana, and in the lower regions he covered nine acres of ground.
4 A mythic river of the lower world.
5 The Danaïdes, who killed their husbands on their wedding night.
6 The crafty king of Corinth, whose punishment in the lower world was to roll up a hill a huge stone which always slipped from his hands before he reached the top.
7 A very fine wine.
8 Metre: Alcaic Strophe.

Soon regal piles will leave little land for plows,[1]
And fishponds stretching wider than Lucrine Lake
    Will everywhere soon meet the gaze, and
        Celibate platan will drive out elm trees;

Soon beds of violets and the myrtle tree,
And all that store delighting the nostrils then
    Will scatter fragrance through the olive
        Groves that bore fruit for their former master;

The laurel, dense with branches, will shutter out
The rays of sun. Not thus the example set
    By Romulus[2] and unshorn Cato,[3]
        Nor by the precepts of elder statesmen.

The list of the possessions they owned was short,
The public wealth great: no private colonnade,
    Marked off with ten-foot rods, did then lie
        Waiting in shade for the northern breezes;

Nor did the laws permit one to scorn chance turf,
Commanding that, at public expense, we should
    Both decorate the towns and also
        Shrines of the gods with new, fresh-hewn marble.[4]

---

[1] Horace inveighs against the luxury of the wealthy Romans, and supports Augustus' policy to foster Italian agriculture, ruined by slave labor, the decay of the peasantry, and the competition of Sicily and Africa.

[2] The founder of Rome.

[3] The elder Cato, the censor, typical of old Roman austerity.

[4] Metre: Alcaic Strophe.

Peace, the sailor prays of the gods when over-
Taken on the open Aegean, and a
Dark cloud hides the moon, with no steady stars on
    Mariners shining:

Peace, entreats the Thracian mad with battle,
Peace, implores the Persian adorned with quiver,
Grosphus[1]—peace which cannot be bought with gems, with
    Gold or with purple.

Royal wealth cannot, nor can consul's lictor
Clear the heart's sad riots, or drive away the
Flying cares which 'round the low, paneled ceilings
    Constantly circle.

He lives well, for whom on his frugal table
Shines his family saltcellar, polished brightly;
Neither fear nor sordid desire disturbs or
    Lightens his slumber.

Why in life so brief do we, still undaunted,
Strive so much? For lands warmed by alien sunshine
Change our own? What exile from homeland ever
    Fled himself also?

Carking care climbs up on the bronze-beaked vessels,
Keeps abreast of galloping troops of horsemen,
Swifter than fleet stags, or the storm cloud driven
    Swiftly by Eurus.[2]

Well contented now is the heart, and loath to
Look beyond, and harsh words would moderate with
Patient laughter; nothing in all respects is
　　Fortunate ever.

Quick death carried off the renowned Achilles,[3]
Age unending withered Tithonus[4] slowly,
And perchance to me what she holds from you, the
　　Glad hour will offer.

Yours, a hundred head of Sicilian cattle
Lowing; yours, a mare to a four-horsed chariot
Reined, and neighing; you dress in wools twice dyed with
　　African purple;

But on me did Fate, never false, bestow a
Modest farm; a breath of the Grecian Muse's
Inspiration gave, and the right to scorn the
　　Envious rabble.[5]

<hr>

[1] Pompeius Grosphus is known only from Horace's Epistles (I, 12), a letter
of introduction to the Iccius of Book I, Ode 29.

[2] Eurus: the southeast wind.

[3] A Greek hero in the Trojan War.

[4] A son of Laomedon, consort of Aurora, and father of Memnon; endowed
with immortality, and changed at last after reaching a decrepit old age into a
cicada.

[5] Metre: Sapphic Strophe.

Why, why with your complaints do you slay my soul?
No pleasure to the gods, neither will of mine
    Is it that you die first, Maecenas,[1]
        Glory and pillar of all my substance.

Ah then, if sudden death snatches you, my life's
Best part, why should the rest of me linger on,
    Since not content nor whole would I live
        After you? That day will bring destruction

To both. For I have sworn the not-faithless oath,
The soldier's oath, that thus we shall go, shall go
    As soon as you pass on before me,
        Comrades prepared for that last, long journey.

For neither shall the fiery Chimaera's[2] breath,
Nor Gyas,[3] hundred-armed, should he rise again,
    Tear me from you: this pleases mighty
        Justice, and thus have the Fates decreed it.

So whether Libra,[4] whether dread Scorpion,[5]
The shape of fear, looks down on my natal hour
    As more predominant, or whether
        Capricorn,[6] tyrant of western waters—

Yet does, in some incredible way, that star
Of ours consent. Against wicked Saturn's beam
    Jove's care flashed back and rescued you and
        Slowed the swift pinions of Death, and thereon

The populace, assembled in theaters,
Three times applauded, raising a happy shout;
    While me—the tree trunk falling on my
        Skull would have killed me, except that Faunus[7]

Struck off the blow—the guardian as he is
Of men of Mercury.[8] Offer sacrifice,
    Remember, too, the shrine you promised;
        We shall be slaying a little lambkin.[9]

[1] Maecenas, though frail in health and suffering from fever and insomnia, clung desperately to life. In an age of astrological superstitions to which Augustus and Maecenas were devoted, Horace here assures his friend that their horoscopes coincide and that they will not be divided in death.

[2] A fabulous monster which breathed forth fire.

[3] A giant, one of the sons of Heaven and Earth.

[4] A propitious sign; the constellation of the Scales.

[5] The influence of this sign was baleful.

[6] A sign of the Zodiac, which the sun enters at the winter solstice.

[7] The god of the woods and country.

[8] Poets were under the protection of Mercury, the god of eloquence and the inventor of the lyre. (See Book I, Ode 10.)

[9] Metre: Alcaic Strophe.

Ivory nor paneled gold
   Upon the ceiling gleams within my dwelling,[1]
Marble beams Hymettian[2]
   Rest not on columns cut in Africa far
Off, nor have I, as the heir
   Unknown of Attalus, possessed the palace,
Neither for me do the well-
   Born ladies of my house weave purple garments.
Faith is mine, a kindly vein
   Of talent, and the wealthy seek me out though
I be poor; the gods above
   I importune for nothing, nor my mighty
Friend for greater wealth assail;
   Content am I with just my Sabine acres.
Day crowds closely after day,
   New moons grow full and then are lost to heaven:
You, upon the edge of death,
   Still let the contract for the marble's cutting;
Mindless of the tomb, you build
   Your villa, and at Baiae[3] push the shore line
Out into the sounding sea,
   Not rich enough with beaches of the mainland.
Nay, more than that, you still remove
   The nearest landmarks of your pauper tenants'
Fields, and greedily you jump
   His boundaries; and he is driven forth, while
Clutching in his toga's fold
   His family gods: the man, his wife, their wretched
Children. Yet no hall awaits

More certainly the wealthy lord than greedy
Orcus'[4] destined end of death.

Then why do you reach out for more? The equal
Earth is opened to receive

The pauper and the sons of kings; nor yet has
Charon,[5] unseduced by gold,

Brought back the sly Prometheus. He holds as
Captive Tantalus and all

The tribe of Tantalus, consents to lift the
Poor man finished with his toil:

When he is called and when not called, he harkens.[6]

[1] Horace contrasts the cares of wealth with the pleasures of the simple life.
[2] From Mount Hymettus in Attica.
[3] A famous Campanian resort near Naples, frequented for its warm baths. Some of the wealthy Romans built their villas out into the water.
[4] God of the infernal regions; Pluto.
[5] Charon: the ferryman of the river Styx in the lower world.
[6] Metre: Trochaic Strophe.

I saw him![1]—Bacchus!—off among distant rocks,
Believe me! saw him teaching the nymphs their songs;
    Posterity, I saw them learning,
        Saw the sharp ears of goat-footed satyrs!

Evoe![2] my spirit trembles anew with fear;
Confusedly my heart filled with Bacchus now
    Exults! Evoe! Oh, spare me, Liber,
        Spare me your thyrsus[3] so greatly dreaded!

It is my right to sing of the Thyades[4]
Untiring, and the fountain that spouted wine,
    To sing of milk that filled the rivers,
        Honey that flowed from the hollow tree trunks,

Of Ariadne,[5] given a crown of stars,
To tell of how the palace of Pentheus[6]
    Was overthrown, and the ungentle
        Thracian Lycurgus[7] was brought to ruin.

You tame the rivers, tame the barbaric sea,
And, moist with wine, you twist in a snaky knot
    Upon remotest peaks, the hair of
        Thracian women, and with no danger.

And when a troop of impious giants climbed
Up steepest heights, clear up to your father's realm,
    You cast back Rhoetus,[8] and with jaw and
        Claws of a terrible lion flung him;

Although you were more suitable, it was said,
For dances, jests, and sport, you were deemed to be
    Not suitable for war; and yet you
        Were just the same in both peace and warfare.

When Cerberus[9] beheld you with golden horn
Adorned, he hurt you not, but with three-forked tongue
    He, harmless, licked at your departing
        Feet and your legs, his tail wagging gently.[10]

[1] Horace pretends to have caught sight of Bacchus and his train on the lonely hillside.

[2] Evoe!, i.e., the cry of the devotees of Bacchus. Liber is Bacchus.

[3] The thyrsus of Bacchus was a pole on the top of which was a fir-cone or vine or ivy leaves. Its touch inspired frenzy.

[4] The bacchantes, the raving women who celebrated the orgies of the god.

[5] A daughter of Minos, king of Crete, who extricated Theseus from the labyrinth, and accompanied him on his return to Greece. He deserted her, however, at Naxos, where Bacchus fell in love with her, and placed her crown among the constellations.

[6] Euripides in the *Bacchae* describes the punishment of King Pentheus of Thebes for his impious resistance to the worship of the new god.

[7] Lycurgus: king of Thrace who attempted to suppress the worship of Bacchus in his kingdom.

[8] Rhoetus: one of the giants who climbed to heaven to do battle with the gods.

[9] The three-headed dog of Pluto that guarded the entrance to the lower world.

[10] Metre: Alcaic Strophe.

Upon[1] no frail or commonplace pinion[2] borne
Shall I, two-formed, be lifted through limpid air,
    A poet-bird past envy, I'll not
        Linger on earth, but shall leave the cities.

I shall not perish, blood of a pauper sire,[3]
Not I whom you invite to your home as guest,
    Esteemed Maecenas; nor shall I by
        Stygian wave be confined or hindered.

Already now the roughening skin shrinks down
Upon my legs; above I become transformed,
    I am a white-winged bird, and through my
        Fingers and shoulders light plumes are sprouting.

More famous than Daedalian Icarus,[4]
I'll view the moaning Bosphorus'[5] shores; a bird
    Of melody, I'll visit Afric
        Gulfs and the Hyperborean meadows.

Me shall the Colchian know, and the Dacian
Who masks his fear of Marsian cohorts, and
    The far-off Scythians,[6] the learned
        Spaniard, the drinker of Rhonish waters.[7]

Let there be absent then from my vacant tomb
All dirges, lamentations, unseemly grief;
    Curb clamor and restrain your mourning:
        Leave out those meaningless, empty honors.[8]

1 Horace prophesies his own immortality. The image of poet-bird has been used by other writers. Both Plato and Euripides use the transformation of poet to swan; and the idea of poet as equivalent to bird has been used by Pindar, Theocritus, and Vergil.

2 The reference here is to Horace's claim of having introduced Greek lyric measures into Rome.

3 Horace calmly admits his humble origin.

4 Daedalus of Athens, builder of the Cretan labyrinth, made wings of wax for himself and son Icarus who, on his flight from Crete, fell into the Aegean Sea.

5 Bosphorus (or Bosporus): the waters between Thrace and Asia Minor, now the Straits of Constantinople.

6 Colchis was a province of Asia, east of the Black Sea. The Dacians were a warlike people in the regions of modern Upper Hungary, Transylvania, and Moldavia. The Marsi were one of the bravest of the Latin peoples. The Scythians were nomadic tribes of the north of Europe and Asia, beyond the Black Sea.

7 Horace means that his monument is his poetry.

8 Metre: Alcaic Strophe.

BOOK III

"Seemly and sweet is death for one's native land." — III, 2

I[1] hate the vulgar crowd, and I hold it off!
Keep sacred silence: songs never heard before,
    As priest and poet of the Muses,
        Now do I sing to the youths and maidens.

The rule of dreaded kings is above their own,
Beyond the kings themselves is the reign of Jove
    In triumph shining o'er the Giants,
        Moving all things with his lifted eyebrow.

Yes, true it is that one man may set his trees
In wider rows, this nobler-born candidate
    Descend upon the Campus,[2] this one
        Better in morals and reputation,

Contend with him; to that one a greater crowd
Of clients throng: impartial Necessity
    Decides the fate of high and lowly,
        While the great urn shakes each name and fortune.

For him above whose impious neck the drawn
Sword hangs, the feasts of Sicily hold no taste
    Of savour, nor do notes of bird songs
        Neither do strains of the cithern lead him

Again to sleep. Soft slumber does not disdain
The rustic's lowly home and his shady bank,
    Nor does it scorn the lovely valley
        Shaken and stirred by the western zephyrs.

117

No troubled sea, nor setting Arcturus' fierce
And stormy rush disquiets the man who longs
    For that which is enough for him, nor
        Yet does the rise of the Kid-star Haedus,

Nor vineyards lashed by hail, nor his trickster farm
With trees complaining now of the rains that fall,
    And now of burning stars that parch the
        Country, and now of the unkind winters.

The fishes feel the narrowing of the seas
From great foundations built in the deep, as here
    The foreman, with his throng of men and
        Finical lord of the land, sinks rubble.

But Fear and Threats climb up to the selfsame place
Where mounts the master, nor does black Care depart
    And leave the brassbound trireme, and she
        Always is sitting behind the horseman.

And what if neither Phrygian marble soothes
My pain, nor robes more bright than a star of red
    Or purple, nor Falernian wines, nor
        Even the sweet-smelling Persian attar:

Why should I build a lofty and new-styled hall
With doors that will arouse only jealousy?
    Why should I change my Sabine valley
        For the more burdening care of riches?[3]

---

    1 The first six odes of Book III constitute a sequence of patriotic odes with an identity of metre and a similarity of theme: the virtue of moral purpose, the rewards of courage, discipline, and fidelity, and praise for the empire of Augustus, who on earth is paralleled with Jove in heaven. They seem to have been written in the years 28–26 B.C.
    2 The forms of popular election were preserved by Augustus, and the voting booths were in the Campus Martius.
    3 Metre: Alcaic Strophe.

Let youth, grown strong and hardy in bitter war,
Learn how to bear strait poverty as a friend,
    And, as a dreaded horseman, learn to
        Vex the fierce Parthians with his spearhead,

And lead his life in perilous deeds beneath
The sky. Well may the wife of the warring king
    Upon the hostile walls, perceiving,
        Sigh out, "Alas!" and her ripe young daughter,

"Let not my royal suitor, unskilled in war,
By touch provoke the bloodthirsty lion there,
    And challenge him whom savage wrath is
        Hurrying on through the midst of slaughter."

Seemly and sweet is death for one's native land:
For Death pursues the man who would flee from him,
    Nor spares the knees and shrinking back of
        Those of our youth unprepared for warfare.

True manhood, unaware of defeat's disgrace,
Shines brightly forth with unsullied honors won,
    Nor takes nor lays aside the fasces
        Under the whim of the public favor.

True manhood tries the way by a path denied
To others, opening heaven to those who do
    Not merit death; it spurns the rabble,
        Scorns the dank earth with its soaring pinion.

There is in faithful silence a sure reward:
The man who spreads abroad Ceres' sacred rites[1]
    I'll not permit beneath the selfsame
        Roof, neither may he in fragile vessel

Set sail with me; ofttimes slighted Jupiter
Has to the guilty added the innocent:
    And Vengeance' limping foot has rarely
        Failed to pursue crime which goes before her.[2]

[1] The Eleusinian mysteries, or secret Roman rites of Ceres and Liber, or any mysteries.
[2] Metre: Alcaic Strophe.

A just and steadfast man with a firm intent,
No wrath of men inciting to evil deeds,
    Nor countenance of threatening despot
        Shakes from his purpose, nor can the South Wind

The restless Adriatic's unquiet lord,
Nor mighty hand of thunderbolt-hurling Jove;
    And if the broken vault of heaven
        Fall, it will fall on a man undaunted.

By this same firmness, Pollux[1] and Hercules,
The traveler bold, strove up to the starry heights;
    With them reclining, mouth empurpled,
        There will Augustus drink deep of nectar.

When you, O Father Bacchus, gained honor thus,
Your tigers bore you, yokes on their willful necks,
    To heaven; thus Quirinus fled from
        Acheron's regions on Mars' swift horses,[2]

Queen Juno having uttered this pleasing speech
To gods in council: "Ilium, Ilium[3]
    A guilty judge has turned to dust—a
        Death-dealing judge[4] and a foreign woman,[5]

The day Laomedon[6] of their bargained pay
Deprived the gods, that day was it forfeited
    To me and to the chaste Minerva—
        Troy with its people and crafty leader.

No longer shines the Spartan adulteress'
Notorious guest, nor yet does the perjured house
    Of Priam still beat back the fighting
        Argives[7] with power of Hector's forces.

This war, by our dissensions so long drawn out,
Has ended. I shall henceforth,[8] because of Mars,
    Renounce my wrath and hatred for my
        Grandson the priestess of Troy gave birth to,[9]

And will admit him into the seats of light,
That he may taste the heavenly nectars there;
    I shall permit that he among the
        Untroubled ranks of the gods be listed.

So long as vast and furious seas shall rage
'Twixt Ilium and Rome, everywhere they go
    Shall happy Roman exiles rule; so
        Long as wild cattle upon the hillock,

Upon the tomb of Paris and Priam stamp,
And beasts there, unmolested, conceal their cubs,
    The gleaming Capitol may stand, and
        Bold Rome give laws to the conquered Persians;

And may she spread her name to the farthest shores;
Where seas between cut Europe from Africa—
    May she be feared from there to where the
        Broad-swelling Nile overflows the cornfields.

It shows more strength to spurn undiscovered gold
The earth conceals, and thus better hid, than with
    Rapacious hand which seizes sacred
        Things, to collect it for human uses.

And wheresoe'er the end of the world was set,
This will she touch with armies that long to see
Which part is where the tropic heats rage,
Which is the region of mist and rainfall.

But on this one condition do I set forth
This fate for warlike Romans, which is that they
Shall not—too dutiful, too faithful!—
Wish to rebuild their ancestral city.

Troy's fortunes, born anew 'neath an evil star,
Shall once again in grievous disaster fall,
With me, Jove's sister and his consort,
Leading the troops of the conquering armies.

Were this bronze bulwark three times to rise again
At Phoebus's command, it would three times fall,
Cut down by my own Greeks, thrice would that
Captured wife weep for her sons and husband."

But strains like these befit not the lightsome lyre:
Toward what, O Muse, do you tend? Cease stubbornly
To thus report the gods' discourses,
Dwarfing great themes with your humble music![10]

1 A famous pugilist, son of Tyndarus and Leda, and brother of Castor, in connection with whom, as the constellation of the Twins (Gemini), he served as a guide to mariners. Used here as an ideal type.

2 There was a legend that Romulus (Quirinus) disappeared in a storm, and was translated to heaven in the chariot of Mars.

3 Troy. The repetition is anadiplosis of strong feeling.

4 Paris, who decided the dispute between Juno, Pallas, and Venus over who should be judged the most beautiful Olympian, gave the golden apple to Venus who promised him Helen of Sparta, the most beautiful woman on earth, as a reward. By carrying her off to Troy, he was the cause of the Trojan War, in which he fell by the arrow of Philoctetes.

5 Juno disdains to name Helen.

6 Apollo and Poseidon served a year with King Laomedon, and built the walls

of Troy; but when the day for payment came, Laomedon sent them off with threats.

[7] The Greeks.

[8] "I shall henceforth" (since Troy is punished): Juno renounces her wrath and her hatred of her grandson Romulus, the son of Mars and Rhea Silvia, or Ilia.

[9] Juno does not deign to mention Rhea Silvia's name.

[10] Metre: Alcaic Strophe.

Descend from Heaven, come now and sing a song,
A long song, Queen Calliope,[1] to the flute,
    Or, if you wish, with clear voice only,
        Or with the lyre or Apollo's cittern.

Do you, too, hear it, or does sweet madness charm
And mock me? Surely I seem to hear and through
    The sacred groves to wander, there where
        Clear-flowing streams and soft breezes enter.

On Voltur[2] in Apulia as a boy
And spent with play, when outside my nurse's door
    I lay in sleep, the storied pigeons
        Softly with freshly plucked leaves concealed me,

Which well might be a marvel to all who dwell
In lofty Acherontia's[3] nest, or live
    On Bantia's[4] high lawns, or in the
        Rich, fertile pastures of low Forentum,

That I should sleep, my body unharmed by bears
Or deadly vipers, covered by sacred leaves
    Of laurel and the gathered myrtle,
        I, a bold child with the gods' protection.

Yours, Muses, I am borne up steep Sabine hills,
Yours, whether cool Praeneste[5] be my retreat,
    Or whether Tibur's gentle slopes, or
        Whether the waters of Baiae please me.

Because I love your springs and your dancing throngs
The fateful tree, the rout at Philippi did
     Not quench my life, nor Palinurus[6]
          Washed by Sicilian wave destroy me.

If only you be with me, I shall attempt
By sea the raging Bosphorus willingly,
     Or go by land where stretch the burning
          Sands of Assyria's desert coast line;

I'll visit Britons, hostile to strangers, and
The happy Concan,[7] drinker of horses' blood,
     I'll visit quiver-hung Geloni,
          Visit the Scythian stream, uninjured.

Great Caesar, too, as soon as the troops have drawn
Their weary cohorts into the town, and he
     His labors seeks to finish, then do
          You from Pierian[8] grot refresh him.

In giving gentle counsel, O kindly ones,
You take delight. We know how he overthrew
     The wicked Titans and their monstrous
          Rout by his swift-falling bolt of thunder,

He who alone rules over the sluggish earth,
The wind-swept sea, the towns, and the gloomy realms
     Of death, the gods, and troops of mortals—
          He rules alone with impartial power.

That frightful brood with faith in their many arms
Had struck a great alarm into mighty Jove,
     Their brothers trying, too, to pile up
          Pelion on top of dark Olympus.[9]

What could Typhoeus,[10] what could robust Mimas,
Or Rhoetus, or Porphyrion, threatening-faced,
    What could Enceladus, the daring
        Thrower of tree trunks, accomplish either

By rushing forth against the resounding shield
Of Pallas? Here stood Vulcan[11] with eagerness,
    Here matron Juno stood, here stood one
        Never to put the bow from his shoulder,

Who bathes his flowing locks in Castalia's dew
So pure, who keeps the thickets of Lycia,
    Who holds and guards his native woodlands—
        Delos' and Patara's god, Apollo!

Force lacking judgment falls of its own gross weight,
The gods advance a disciplined force to might
    Still greater; likewise they abhor the
        Forces that move in the mind toward mischief.

The hundred-handed Gyas[12] to what I say
Is witness, and Orion notorious
    Assailant of the chaste Diana,
        He who was tamed by her virgin arrow.

Vexed Earth laments her monsters, her offspring sent
By thunderbolt to Orcus, that ghastly realm;
    Swift flame has not consumed Mount Aetna
        Superimposed on the fires below her,

Nor has the vulture set as a guard on sin
Gone from the lustful Tityos'[13] liver yet;
    As for Pirithoüs[14] the lover—
        Three hundred chains even yet restrain him![15]

1 The Muse of poetry.

2 A mountain near Venusia.

3 A small town in Lucania.

4 Another town; also, Forentum.

5 A town of Latium, famed for the beauty of its roses, for its nuts, and still more for its temple of Fortune and the oracle connected with it. It was high and cool.

6 Nothing is known of Horace's escape from shipwreck near the Lucanian promontory of Palinurus named from Aeneas' pilot.

7 The Concans were a savage Spanish tribe.

8 Pieria, in Thrace, was said to be a haunt of the Muses. Here the Pierian grotto is used figuratively as literary leisure.

9 Pelion and Olympus: mountains in Thessaly, of great height. Olympus was regarded as the seat of the gods.

10 Typhoeus, etc., were giants.

11 The Fire God.

12 A giant with one hundred arms.

13 Tityos had insulted Diana.

14 Pirithoüs, with Theseus, attempted to carry off Proserpina.

15 Metre: Alcaic Strophe.

We have believed that, thundering from the sky,
Jove reigns; a present god will Augustus be
    When he has added to our realm the
        Troublesome Persians and stubborn Britons.

Lives there a man, a soldier of Crassus[1] once,
Yet now a shameful husband with foreign bride;
    The Marsians and Apulians (oh,
        Shame on our Senate, our altered morals!)

Grown old in arms of fathers-in-law, our foes
'Neath Persian king, forgetting their shields, their name,
    Their garb, eternal Vesta's fire, while
        Jove and the city of Rome are standing?

The prescient mind of Regulus[2] dreaded this,
Dissenting from the odious terms of peace
    And drawing from such precedent an
        Omen of ruin for future ages,

If captive youth, unworthy of pity, were
Not left to die. "I saw it myself," he said,
    "Our standards nailed to Punic temples,
        Arms torn from soldiers, and with no bloodshed.

I saw myself the arms of our citizens,
Free men, turned 'round and bound at their backs, saw gates
    No longer closed, saw fields which once our
        Soldiers had ravaged now cultivated.

No doubt the soldier ransomed by gold will then
Return the braver? You are but adding loss
    To shame; when wool is stained with dye, it
        Never regains its departed colors,

Nor does true valor, once it is gone, desire
To be restored to unworthy men. Yes, if
    A deer set free from thickets fights, then
        So will that soldier be brave who trusted

Himself to faithless foes and, with arms bound back
Behind him, dully suffered the lash and feared
    To die—he in a second war then,
        He is the one who will crush Phoenicians!

That man, not knowing how to preserve his life,
Confounded peace with war. Oh, the shame of it!
    O mighty Carthage, lifted higher,
        Built upon Italy's shameful downfall!"

The story still is told how he put aside,
As one deprived of citizen's rights, his chaste
    Wife's kiss, his little sons; and grimly
        Turned to the ground kept his manly visage,

Till he could make the faltering fathers firm
By counsel never given to others, and
    Till he, through midst of mourning friends, could
        Speed his departure, a noble exile.

For though he knew full well what the torturer
Barbaric was preparing for him, he pushed
    Aside his relatives, the crowd that
        Would have delayed him in his returning,

And left as though some tedious business deal
Of clients had been settled, and now he toward
   The pastures of Venafrum[3] or toward
      Spartan Tarentum his course were bending.[4]

[1] Thousands of Romans had been taken prisoners after the defeat of Crassus' army by the Parthians at Carrhae in Mesopotamia in 53 B.C. Some of them had married Parthian women and served in the Parthian armies.

[2] M. Atilius Regulus, the celebrated Roman consul, was taken prisoner by the Carthaginians in the first Punic War. He was sent by them to the Roman Senate to treat for peace, or, failing that, for an exchange of prisoners; but he advised the Senate to reject both propositions.

[3] Venafrum and Tarentum are mentioned as typical holiday resorts.

[4] Metre: Alcaic Strophe.

Though guiltless you may be of your fathers' sins,
You shall atone, O Roman, until at last
    You have restored the fanes, the falling
        Shrines of the gods and their smoke-blacked statues.

Because you hold yourselves less than gods, you rule:
From them trace all beginning, to them each end.
    The gods, neglected, have brought down on
        Sorrowing Italy much misfortune.

Already twice Monaeses[1] has thrown us back,
Pacorus'[2] horde has rudely subdued our force,
    Our ill-timed thrusts, and grin that they have
        Added our spoils to their petty collars.

The Ethiopian and the Dacian tribes
Almost destroyed our city engaged in strife,
    The one more dreaded for its fleet, the
        Other more skillful with flying arrows.

This generation, fruitful of crime, has fouled
Our marriage beds, the blood of our race, our homes;
    And from this source derived has ruin
        Poured through our land and upon our people.

The ripened maiden revels in being taught
Ionic dances; trained in coquettish arts,
    Already she is planning guilty
        Loves even now in her tender girlhood.

She later at the feasts of her husband seeks
For younger loves, nor picks one to whom she may,
  When all the lights have been removed, with
    Eagerness give the forbidden pleasures,

But rises openly when some trader calls—
And not without her husband's awareness why!—
  Some Spanish vessel's captain, any
    Freehanded buyer of her dishonor.

Not from such parents sprung was our noble youth
Who stained the sea's smooth surface with Punic blood,
  Felled Pyrrhus,[3] great Antiochus,[4] and
    Vanquished dread Hannibal's force with slaughter:

But manly sons of country-bred soldiery,
Those taught to turn the sod with their Sabine hoes,
  To cut and carry logs to please the
    Whim of a rigorous mother's judgment,

Until the sun should alter the mountains' shades,
And from the weary oxen remove the yoke,
  Thus, with his chariot departing,
    Ushering in the most welcome hour.

Ah, what does this injurious age not harm?
Our parents' life-span, worse than our grandsires' time,
  Bore us who are more worthless, and soon
    We shall produce still more sinful offspring.[5]

---

[1] A king of the Parthians.

[2] A son of Orodes, king of Parthia, the conqueror of Crassus.

[3] King of Epirus, an enemy of the Romans, was defeated at Beneventum, 275 B.C.

[4] Antiochus the Great, a king of Syria, was defeated at Magnesia, 190 B.C.

[5] Metre: Alcaic Strophe.

Why weep, Asteria,[1] why weep for him whom Spring's
Brightening zephyrs will bring back to you, rich with wares
    Of Bithynia—Gyges[2]
        Of unshakeable loyalty?

He, by winds from the south driven to Oricum,[3]
South winds following close after the Goat's wild star—
    Now lies, passing the cold nights
        Sleepless, not without many tears.

The sly messenger[4] comes of his disquieted
Hostess, telling him how sad Chloe is and sighs,
    How she burns with your own fires—
        Tempting him in a thousand ways:

How a treacherous wife urged on the credulous
Proetus—many the false charges she made to him!—
    And impelled him to speed death
        For the too chaste Bellerophon;

Tells of Peleus sent almost to Tartarus[5]
As he, pure, fled the Magnesian Hippolyta;
    And, with guileful intent, she
        Tells him stories that prompt to sin.

But in vain: he is more deaf than Icarian
Rocks as, innocent still, he hears her words. But you—
    You take care lest Enipeus,
        Your good neighbor, please you too much,

Although no one else knows how to control a horse
So well, none so observed out on the Martian Field,
    Nor does anyone else so
        Swiftly swim down the Tuscan stream.

But when twilight descends, close up your house, nor look
When his plaintive flute sounds, down at the streets below;
    And though often he calls you
        Cruel, obdurate still remain.[6]

[1] The severity of the preceding odes is now relieved by this pretty idyl. Asteria is a girl's name, meaning "Like a star."

[2] A beautiful youth.

[3] Gyges has been driven into the harbor of Oricum in Epirus by autumn storms, and there impatiently awaits the opening of the next season's navigation to cross the Adriatic to Italy.

[4] Chloe's messenger tells him of how Bellerophon rejected the advances of Anteia, the wife of his host Proetus, and of how she thereupon slandered him to her husband, who tried to bring about his death. The story of Peleus and Hippolyta, wife of Acastus, king of Magnesia in Thessaly, is similar.

[5] The infernal regions.

[6] Metre: Fourth Asclepiadean.

III, 8

What can I be doing on March's calends,[1]
I, a bachelor? What do these flowers mean, and
Burners full of incense, and coals laid here on
    Freshly cut altars:

You, though learned in lore of both tongues, yet wonder?
Almost done to death by a falling tree, I
Promised then to Liber a dainty feast and
    White little he-goat.

This day, festive at the returning season,
Shall remove the cork of the pitch-sealed vessel
Placed back there so as to inhale the smoke when
    Tullus was consul.

Take, Maecenas, one hundred cups to honor
Now your friend's escape, and endure the watchful
Lamps till daylight; far away let there be all
    Uproar and passion!

Lay aside your care for the city's welfare,
Come! the Dacian Cotiso's[2] host is fallen;
Hostile Medes, divided, with mournful weapons
    Turn on each other.

Tamed, our ancient foe of the Spanish border,[3]
Cantaber, and slave to the chain at last; the
Scythians, their bows all unstrung, consider
    Leaving their prairies.

Caring not, for once, if the people suffer,
Spare too much concern; as a private person
Gladly seize the gifts of the present hour; leave
    Serious matters.[4]

---

[1] On the calends of March (i.e., the first day in March) married people and lovers celebrated the festival of the Matronalia in honor of Mars.

[2] King of the Dacians. He was defeated by Augustus' lieutenant Lentulus.

[3] Spain was the first province to be entered by the Romans, but was the last to be subdued.

[4] Metre: Sapphic Strophe.

He: While I still was your best-beloved,[1]
        And when no other youth, favored above myself,
        Laid his arms 'round your fair, white neck,
        Then I flourished with joy, more than a Persian king.

She: While you burned not for someone else,
        Nor did Lydia rank second to Chloe's place,
        I was Lydia much-renowned,
        I bloomed famous and bright, more than Rome's Ilia.

He: For me now, Thracian Chloe rules,
        Taught in measures most sweet, skilled with the cittern's strings,
        For whose sake I'd not fear to die,
        If the Fates would but spare still her surviving soul.

She: For me, Calais burns with love,
        Thurine Ornytus' son, burns with an answered fire,
        And for him would I perish twice,
        If the Fates would spare him, spare still that lad unharmed.

He: What if olden love comes again
        And drives us, now apart, under a yoke of bronze;
        Fair-haired Chloe be cast away,
        And to Lydia, scorned, now my door opens wide?

She: Though more bright than a star is he,
        And you lighter than cork and far stormier
        Than the fierce Adriatic Sea,
        Yet with you would I live, gladly with you I'd die![2]

[1] Horace(?) and Lydia, or the lover's quarrel.
[2] Metre: Second Asclepiadean.

Though[1] you dwelt by the Don,[2] Lisa, and drank of it,
And were wed to a harsh husband, you still might weep
To expose me, outstretched prone by your cruel doors,
    To Aquilo's sharp, native winds.

Do you hear the gate creak, hear how the planted trees
In your pretty courtyard groan in the northern blasts,
And how Jupiter now out of a cloudless sky
    With ice glazes the fallen snow?

Put your pride down—most displeasing to Venus, that!—
Lest the cord should fly back with the reverting wheel:
No Penelope stern, harsh to her suitors still,
    Did your Tuscany sire beget.

O though not all my gifts, neither my prayers, nor the
Pallor, violet-tinged, staining your lover's cheeks,
Nor your spouse wounded sore by a Pierian girl
    Moves you, spare yet your suppliants;

Lady, you are no more soft than the rigid oak,
Neither are you at heart gentler than Moorish snakes:
Not forever will my body be lying here
    And enduring the rains of heaven![3]

---

[1] Lament of the excluded lover before the door of his mistress.
[2] A river in Sarmatia (Russia).
[3] Metre: Third Asclepiadean.

Mercury, for you were the master whose well-
Taught Amphion[1] conjured the stones by singing;
You too, shell, so skilled with your seven strings in
    Sounding back music,

Neither tuneful were you nor pleasing once, but
Welcome now in temples, at rich men's feasts—oh,
Teach me strains which Lyda[2] may turn at last her
    Obstinate ear to,

She who, like some three-year-old filly, frisks on
Widespread fields and fears to be touched, and knowing
Nothing yet of nuptials, she still is not quite
    Ripe for a husband.

Tigers you can lead, and attendant forests,
You can stay the courses of rapid rivers;
To your wiles the guard of the monstrous palace,
    Cerberus, yielded,

Though a hundred serpents protect his dreadful
Head, and from his triple-tongued mouth a constant
Stream of foulest breath keeps on pouring out, and
    Venomous matter.

Even grim Ixion[3] and Tityos[4] did
Smile reluctantly; and the urn stood dry a
Moment while, with melody sweet, you charmed the
    Danaïd daughters.

Now let Lyda hear of the virgins' crime, their
Well-known punishment, and the empty jar whose
Waters disappear through the bottom, and the
    Long-deferred doom which

Waits to punish crimes, yes, waits still in Orcus.
Wicked maids! (for what worse could they have done?) oh,
Wicked maids, who could with the ruthless blade thus
    Murder their bridegrooms!

Only one of many was worthy of the
Torch of marriage, splendidly lying to her
Perjured father, she was a noble maiden
    Famous through ages:

"Rise!" she cried instead to her youthful bridegroom,
"Rise, lest from a hand which you do not fear, too
Long a sleep be given; my father and my
    Villainous sisters

Foil, who like wild lionesses that chance on
Calves, tear them, alas! one by one. I am more
Merciful, for I shall not slay you, neither
    Hold you imprisoned.

Now with cruel chains may my father load me,
Since I spared through kindness my wretched husband;
Or, to the Numidians' far-off country
    Send me by shipboard.

Go, where'er your feet and the breezes take you,
While the night and Venus still favor going,
Go with happy omen; a mournful memory
    Carve on my tombstone."[5]

---

[1] He reared the "song-built towers and gates" (Alfred, Lord Tennyson, "Tiresias") of Thebes.

[2] "The name merely supplies a motive and setting for Horace's treatment of the more pleasing side of the myth (according to Shorey, *Horace—Odes and Epodes,* 356): Danaus, descendant of Io the daughter of Inachus, returned with fifty daughters from Egypt to his ancestral home, Argos. Constrained to marry his daughters to their cousins, the sons of Aegyptus, who had pursued them from Egypt, he bound the girls to assassinate their husbands on the bridal night. Hypermnestra alone spared her husband Lynceus, and became the ancestress of the line of Danae, Perseus, and Hercules. . . . Horace's readers were familiar with the statues of the Danaïdes that stood between the columns of the porticus of the temple of Apollo on the Palatine Hill." Pindar, Aeschylus, Ovid, and others have used this story.

[3] Ixion: king of the Lapithae in Thessaly, and father of Pirithoüs. Jupiter hurled him into Tartarus, where he was bound fast to a perpetually revolving wheel.

[4] Tityos: see II, 14.

[5] Metre: Sapphic Strophe.

142

It[1] is not for wretched maidens to give love play, neither may they
Drown in sweet wine all their troubles; they instead must be in terror
Of an uncle's stinging tongue-lash.

Your wool basket, Neobule, and your loom, your inclination
For Minerva's busy tasks Cupid, light-winged, steals, and the beauty
Of that youth, Lipara's[2] Hebrus;

When he once has bathed oiled shoulders in the Tiber, he is better
As a horseman than Bellerophon himself; nor is he vanquished
In the boxing or the footrace.

He is likewise skilled in striking deer that flee across the open
When the herd has been excited, and is quick to draw the boar out
That is lurking in the thicket.[3]

[1] This is the complaint of the lovelorn Neobule who cannot spin for thinking about the bright beauty of the young athlete, Hebrus. The girl is talking to herself.
[2] Lipara was a small volcanic island on the northeast coast of Sicily.
[3] Metre: the Lesser Ionic.

Fount of Bandusia,[1] shining more bright than glass,
Worth the sweetest of wine not without garlands crowned,[2]
   On the morrow a young kid
      Will be given you, one whose brow

Swollen with his first horns marks him for love and fight;
In vain: for with his blood, crimson blood shall he dye
   All your icy cold streams; the
      Offspring, he, of a wanton flock.

You the blazing Dog Star's season of savage heat
Is unable to touch; and to the straying sheep,
   Oxen tired from the plowshare,
      You give welcome and cooling rest.

You shall also become one of our honored streams
When I tell of the oak anchored upon the rocks,
   Ilex crowning the cavern
      Whence your talkative waters leap.[3]

---

[1] This exquisite and musical ode is a famous one. A medieval document mentions a *fons Bandusinus* near Horace's birthplace, Venusia; and tradition or Horace himself may have transferred the name to a spring or little waterfall on his Sabine estate.

[2] Wine was poured into the fountain with the flowers.

[3] Metre: Fourth Asclepiadean.

III, 14

Just like Hercules, Caesar comes,[1] O people,
Who, so it was said, sought the laurel bought by
Death; he comes a victor from Spanish coast lines,
    Seeking his home gods.

Let his wife rejoice in her peerless husband,
Go and sacrifice to the righteous gods; our
Famous leader's sister go forth; adorned with
    Suppliant fillets

Mothers, too, of sons now returned in safety,
And of maidens. You, O you youths and brides but
Newly married, carefully now refrain from
    Words of ill omen.

This day, truly festive for me, shall drive black
Care away, and neither rebellion shall I
Fear, nor death by violence while our Caesar
    Rules every region.

Go, boy, seek out perfume and leafy garlands
And a cask that calls back the Marsic combat,
If by chance a jug has escaped the raids of
    Spartacus,[2] roving.

Bid clear-voiced Neaera[3] to hurry now, and
In a knot to bind her myrrh-scented hair; but
If delay is caused by her hateful porter,[4]
    Why, come away then!

Whitening hair[5] makes softer the dispositions
Eager once for strife and for headstrong quarrels;
I should not have borne this in youth's hot blood, when
    Plancus[6] was consul![7]

1 This ode celebrates the return of Augustus in 24 B.C. from an absence of three years in the West, where he had been engaged in subduing the Cantabrians and settling the affairs of the provinces. He had been ill for some months at Tarraco, and considerable anxiety had been felt at Rome.

2 A Thracian gladiator, who carried on the war of the gladiators against the Romans.

3 A woman's name.

4 The porters refused to admit the messenger.

5 Horace was forty-one, but prematurely gray.

6 L. Munatius Plancus was consul in 42 B.C., the year of the campaign of Philippi. The fever in Horace's blood had cooled, along with that in the body politic.

7 Metre: Sapphic Strophe.

Put an end to your wantonness,[1]
    Who are Ibycus' wife, pauper though he may be;
Leave your scandalous deeds at last,
    Who are fitter by far now for a timely grave;
Cease to frolic among the maids
    And to scatter a cloud over the shining stars.
That which may become Pholoe
    Is not suited to you, Chloris; your daughter can
Storm the homes of young men like some
    Thyad[2] roused by the drum—better for her than you!
Love for Nothus[3] drives her to frisk
    Like a playful young kid; wools of the noted flocks
Shorn near famous Luceria[4]
    Are more fitting for you—not the guitar, nor the
Crimson bloom of the rose, nor casks
    Emptied, drunk to the dregs, old woman that you are![5]

[1] The unpleasant theme of I, 25, and IV, 13.
[2] A bacchante.
[3] For any roué.
[4] A city of Apulia.
[5] Metre: Second Asclepiadean.

Well enough had a bronze tower and doors of oak
And a surly watchdog's vigilant guard secured
Closely held Danaë,[1] keeping her prisoned there
    Safe from night-roving paramours,

Had not Jupiter laughed, Venus and he both laughed
At the guard of the maid, trembling Acrisius;
For the way would be safe, open and safe, they knew
    When the god changed himself to gold.

Gold loves making its way right through the midst of guards,
Loves to break through rock walls, abler than lightning bolt;
Thus the Argive seer's house,[2] all on account of gold,
    Perished, plunged in catastrophe.

Macedonia's man[3] broke open city gates,
Broke them open with gold; undermined rival kings,
Bribing them with his gifts; presents ensnare even
    Fierce commanders of sailing ships.

Care and hunger for more follow increasing wealth,
Thus with reason have I shrunk back from lifting a
Far-conspicuous head, O my Maecenas, you
    Who are knighthood's great ornament.

For the more that a man shall have denied himself,
All the more shall he then gain from the gods; I, stripped,
Seek the campfires of those asking for nothing; and
    Would desert from the side of wealth.

Much more splendid am I, lord of a scorned estate,
Than if I, were it said, hid in my barns all that
The Apulian reaps, sturdy, unwearied; for
    Then would I, amidst wealth, be poor.

Just a stream crystal clear, wooded acres a few,
A firm faith in my fields; my joy is greater far
Than his glittering lot, though unknown to the great
    Lord of Africa's fertile plains.

Though Calabrian bees bring me no honey here,
Nor in Formian jars mellows the languid, sweet
Laestrygonian[4] wine, nor do thick fleeces grow
    In the pastures of Gaul[5] for me;

Yet is poverty's pinch still far away from me;
Nor, if I should wish more, would you refuse to give.
It is better that I stretch out small revenues
    By restriction of my desire,

Than if I were to join Alyattes' domain[6]
To the Phrygian fields. They who seek much lack much;
Well for him to whom God has, with a sparing hand,
    Given that which is just enough![7]

---

[1] The myth of Danaë is used here as a symbol of the power of gold and a preface to moralizing on the superior happiness of contentment.

Acrisius, king of Argos, fearing the fulfillment of an oracle that his grandson should slay him, shut up his daughter Danaë from all suitors. But Jupiter found access to her in a shower of gold, and she became the mother of Perseus. References to this myth abound throughout ancient and modern literature—some of them quite beautiful. Horace's cynical interpretation, however, seems to have been a commonplace.

[2] The Argive seer: Amphiaraus, whose wife Eriphyle was bribed by Polynices with the necklace of Harmonia to persuade her husband to join the expedition of the Seven against Thebes, in which he met the death he had foreseen. Their son Alcmaeon slew Eriphyle to avenge his father, and was haunted by the furies

of his mother like Orestes. The "house" was thus like that of Pelops (I, 6), a theme of tragedy.

3 Philip of Macedon, father of Alexander the Great, is reputed to have said that any fortress could be taken that could be reached by an ass laden with gold.

4 Formian. Formiae is said to have been the capitol of the Laestrygones.

5 Cisalpine Gaul, noted for fine white wool.

6 According to Herodotus, Croesus (noted for his wealth) was the son of Alyattes, king of Lydia.

7 Metre: Third Asclepiadean.

III, 17

O Aelius,[1] from Lamus's ancient line
So nobly born, since both elder Lamias
    And their posterity were named from
        Him, it is told through recording annals;

From him you trace your origin, who was first
To hold the walls of Formiae, it is said,
    And reigned along the Liris[2] flowing
        Over the banks of the nymph Marica,

Wide-ruling lord—tomorrow a storm sent down
By Eurus[3] will with many a leaf bestrew
    The grove, the shore with useless seaweed—
        That is, unless the old crow, predictor

Of rain, deceives me. So, while you can, pile up
Dry wood: tomorrow you will with wine and two-
    Months' pig attend your household god, with
        All of your servants released from labor.[4]

---

[1] L. Aelius Lamia, the friend of I, 26, and probably the consul of 2 A.D. Under the empire (says Shorey, *Horace—Odes and Epodes*, 373) the Lamiae became types of ancient nobility. Lamia apparently is at his seaside villa. Horace in jest traces his friend's pedigree back to Homer's cannibal king Lamus, and bids him, since a storm is brewing, get in his firewood and prepare to 'loaf and invite his soul.'

[2] The quiet Liris near its mouth overflows in marshes at Minturnae, where the Italian nymph Marica (sometimes identified with Circe) was worshipped.

[3] The southeast wind.

[4] Metre: Alcaic Strophe.

III, 18

Faunus,[1] you the lover of fleeing nymphs, move
Gently through my boundaries and my sunny
Farm, and gently go on your way again, still
    Kind to my younglings,

If a tender kid, when the year is ended
Dies for you, and if to the goblet (Venus'
Comrade) wines lack not, and the ancient altar
    Smokes with much incense.

All the cattle sport on the grassy field, when
Comes again your day, the December nones;[2] while
With the quiet oxen the festive village
    Idles on meadows.

'Midst the fearless lambkins the wolf goes wand'ring;
Woodlands strew their leaves for your rustic carpet;
On the hated[3] earth the rejoicing peasant
    Stamps triple measure.[4]

---

[1] Addressed to Faunus, guardian of the flocks. The Faunalia occurred on February 13; however, Horace here seems to refer to a local festival in December.

[2] The nones were the fifth day in every month of the year except March, May, July, and October, in which it was the seventh (so called because it was the ninth day before the ides).

[3] "Hated" because of the toil she exacts. Slaves worked in chains on the great estates; however, here the Latin word *fossor* means merely "peasant."

[4] Metre: Sapphic Strophe.

Of how long after Inachus[1]
    Codrus came, who was not fearful to die for his
Country, Aeacus' stock you tell;
    And the wars that were waged, fighting near sacred Troy.
But what price we must pay for Chian
    And who will, with his fire, heat us our water, or
Who will lend us his house, and when
    I'll get over this Pelignian[2] cold—of these,
Silence! Then to the crescent moon,
    Boy, one cup quickly give, one to the midnight hour,
Give Murena, the augur, one:
    With three ladles or nine, fitly our cups are mixed;
He who loves the unevenly
    Numbered Muses, the rapt bard, will ask three times three;
More than three will the Grace forbid
    Us to touch, fearing brawls; she, hand-in-hand with her
Naked sisters, denies us more.
    I enjoy being mad. Why cease the notes of the
Berecynthian flute?[3] And why,
    Why hangs silent the pipe? Why hangs the silent lyre?
As for me, I hate grudging hands:
    Scatter roses; and let envious Lycus hear
All our riotous noisy din,
    And our neighbor so ill-matched with old Lycus there.
Little Rhoda, grown ripe, seeks you,

Seeks for you, Telephus,[4] bright as the evening star
With your thick-growing, glossy hair:
As for me, a slow love burns for my Glycera.[5]

[1] The first king of Argos; and Codrus was the semimythical last king of Athens. "You prattle of Inachus and ancient history," Horace cries to a learned friend, "when the important thing is what brand of Chian shall we buy, and at whose house shall we dine together tonight." Then he pictures in his imagination how it will be, giving out toasts, instructing how to mix the water with the wine, bidding them all make merry until the envious old neighbor, ill-mated with a beautiful young wife, hears their revelry.

[2] The Peligni, a people of central Italy and located high in the Apennine Mountains, were proverbially cold.

[3] Cf. I, 18. The Berecynthian flute, the *tibia*, was orgiastic.

[4] Cf. I, 13.

[5] Metre: Second Asclepiadean.

Don't you see how dangerous it may be to
Take a Moorish lioness' cubs away, O
Pyrrhus?[1] Soon, a cowardly spoiler, you will
    Flee the rough battle,

When through blocking throngs of our youths she passes,
Seeking out her peerless Nearchus; whether
He fall prize to you rather than to her, yet
    Mighty the contest.

In the meantime, while you draw forth swift arrows,
While she whets her terrible teeth, the umpire
Of the fight is said to have placed the palm branch
    Under his naked

Foot, and to be fanning with gentle breeze his
Shoulder where, outspread, lie his perfumed locks; as
Fair as Nireus[2] or that youth[3] snatched up from
    Fountainy[4] Ida.[5]

---

[1] Take care, Pyrrhus. Your furious rival will rush on you like a lioness robbed of her whelps. Meanwhile Nearchus, the object of your strife, stands unconcerned, letting the breeze fan his perfumed locks, fair and as cool as marble.

[2] "Nireus was the fairest man that to fair Ilion came" (see Homer's *Iliad*, trans. by George Chapman, II, 72.)

[3] Ganymede, the cupbearer of Jupiter.

[4] Mount Ida, a high mountain in Phrygia near Troy.

[5] Metre: Sapphic Strophe.

O[1] born with me in Manlius' consulship,
My faithful wine jar, whether you bring complaints
    Or jests or quarreling, frantic loves, or
        Whether you bring us an easy slumber,

For whatsoever use you may store this fine
Choice Massic, you deserve to be opened on
    This lucky day; come down; pour out your
        Mellower wine at Corvinus' bidding.

He will not, though in Socrates' speeches steeped,
Be churl enough to slight you; for it is told
    That even stern old Cato's[2] valor
        Ofttimes grew warm with a cup of vintage.

To dispositions normally strict you touch
A gentle spur; anxieties you reveal
    With your relaxing juice, you bare the
        Cares of the wise and their secret planning;

You lead back hope and strength to our troubled minds,
And horns of plenty give to the needy man
    Who, after you, quakes not at angry
        Helmets of kings or the arms of soldiers.

You, Liber, and glad Venus (if she will come),
The Graces, loath to loosen their girdles, shall
    With living lamps prolong the fun till
        Phoebus, returning, puts all the stars out.[3]

¹ To a wine jar born with Horace in the year 65 B.C., and now to be opened in honor of (M. Valerius Messala) Corvinus. Messala was a student at Athens in 42 B.C., with Horace and Marcus Cicero. After Philippi, he declined the leadership of the remnant of the republican party and joined the triumvirs. At the time of the peace of Brundisium, he left the service of Antony for that of Octavian, on whose side he was found at Actium. He was consul in 31 B.C., and was granted a triumph for victories over the Acquitanians in 27 B.C. Thereafter he devoted himself to his law practice and lettered ease. He was the Maecenas of the circle of Tibullus.

² Cf. II, 15.

³ Metre: Alcaic Strophe.

Virgin goddess,[1] keeper of hills and woodlands,
Who, when called three times, hear young wives in travail,
And from very death do you rescue them—oh,
    Goddess of three forms:[2]

Let this pine be yours which o'erhangs my villa,
And at each year's close, may I do it honor
Gladly with the blood of a boar[3] that dreams of
    Slashing out slantwise.[4]

---

[1] Dedication of a pine tree, at Horace's villa, to Diana, queen of the woods.
[2] As Luna, Diana, and Hecate. Her image at the crossways had three faces.
[3] On account of the position of its tusks, the boar strikes sidewise.
[4] Metre: Sapphic Strophe.

If[1] to the sky you lifted your upturned palms
At each new moon, my country-bred Phidyle,[2]
    Appeased your household gods with this year's
        Fruitage, with incense, and greedy piglet,

Destroying Africus[3] shall your fruitful vine
Not feel, nor crops the withering Robigo,[4]
    Nor tender sucklings know a sickly
        Time in the fruit-bearing autumn season.

The fated victim grazes among the oak
And ilex there on snow-covered Algidus,[5]
    Or grows in Alban pastures, and shall
        Stain with its neck's blood the pontiff's axes:

You have no need, with slaughter of two-year sheep
To importune the lesser divinities,[6]
    The little images you crown with
        Rosemary bloom and a sprig of myrtle.

If guiltless be the hand that has touched the shrine,
By costly sacrifice no more fitly does
    It soothe offended gods than just by
        Purified grain and a salty crackling.[7]

[1] Horace, Epicurean and student of Greek philosophy, "tells the farmer's little girl that the gods will love her, though she has only a handful of salt to give them." (John Ruskin, "Queen of the Air," 48).
[2] Phídylè, three syllables.
[3] The wind from Africa, the sirocco.
[4] Blight was regularly worshipped as a deity to be propitiated.
[5] See I, 21.
[6] The little images of the *lares* (the household gods), in her case of wood.
[7] Metre: Alcaic Strophe.

Though more rich than the untouched wealth
  Of the Arabs or of sumptuous India,
You be granted the right to fill
  With your stones all the Apulian and Tuscan seas,
If ill-boding Necessity
  At the tops of your roofs fixes her spikes of steel,[1]
You shall not free your mind from fear
  Nor your head from the noose cast by the net of death.
Better far do the Scythians live,
  The plain-dwellers whose carts, after their manner, draw
Forth their moveable homes; the stern
  Getans also for whom measureless acres bear
Free fruits common to all, and corn,
  Neither care they to till longer than just one year,
And a substitute takes the place
  Of one done with his tasks, serving on equal terms.
There a woman is calm and kind
  To her stepsons who lack mothering from their own,
And no dowered wife rules her spouse,
  Neither puts she her trust in a spruce paramour;
For her dot is her parents' worth,
  And her chastity firm, fearing another man,
Resolute in her faithful vow:
  There the crime is to sin; dying the price thereof.
O whoever would put an end
  To our bloodshed and strife (wicked our civil strife!)
If as Father of Cities he
  Shall seek thus to be named underneath statues, then

Let him (famed to posterity)
  Dare to check uncontrolled liberty: since, alas,
Our shame! virtue alive we hate,
  Which we jealously seek once it is gone from sight.
What will sad lamentations gain
  If the crime is not checked, cut down by punishment?
What can laws without morals do?
  Vain rules, if neither that part of the world inclosed
By the heat of the torrid zones,
  Nor that side of the earth bordering Boreas,[3]
Nor hard snow on the ground can drive
  Off the trader? Rough seas skilled seamen overcome;
For, since poverty is disgrace,
  It commands us to do anything, and endure;
Yet the arduous path of worth,[4]
  Virtue's difficult path, poverty oft forsakes.
Either then to the Capitol[5]
  Where the clamor invites and our supporting throng,
Or else down to the nearest sea
  Let us send all our gems, stones, and our useless gold,
They the cause of our greatest ills—
  If we really repent all our enormities.
Elements of depraved desire
  Must be rubbed from our thought; furthermore, minds too soft
Must by rigorous discipline
  Then be molded anew. Weakly the freeborn youth
Does not know how to sit a horse,
  And is fearful to hunt; more skilled is he if you
Bid him play with the Grecian hoop,
  Or perhaps with the dice, which is against the law;
While his father's false, perjured faith
  Fools his partner in business and his guests, as he
Makes all haste to store up his wealth
  For his unworthy heir. Truly his shameless wealth

Grows, yet something is lacking still,
  Something—I know not what!—from his curtailed estate.[6]

---

[1] The image here is somewhat confused, but the meaning seems to be "You build, but the last nail will be driven by destiny." The "tops of the roofs" would then seem to mean "in (or into) the topmost gable."

[2] The Hindu death-god Yama flings a noose.

[3] The mountain wind from the north.

[4] Proverbially steep. Cf. William Shakespeare's *Hamlet*, Act I, scene 3: "Show me the steep and thorny way to heaven."

[5] To dedicate them to Jupiter amid the applause of the crowd.

[6] Metre: Second Asclepiadean.

Whither, Bacchus,[1] do you transport
    Me now, filled full of you? Or toward what woods, what caves
Am I swiftly led on by this
    Strange, new impulse? By what caverns shall I be heard,
Musing great Caesar's endless praise,
    How to set it 'mid stars and in the plan of Jove?
Something notable, new, unsung
    By another, I'll sing. Just as the Eviad,[2]
Sleepless, looks from her mount, amazed
    On the Hebrus[3] and Thrace, glistening white with snow,
And on Rhodope,[4] trodden by
    The barbarian foot; so in my wandering
It delights me to gaze with rapt
    Wonderment at the lone groves and the riverbanks.
Lord of Naiads and Bacchae, strong
    To uproot with their hands even the lofty ash,
Nothing humble or mean shall I
    Sing, or likely to die. Rapturous peril this,
O Lenaeus,[5] to follow that
    God who circles his brow, binds it with young, green vine![6]

---

[1] Horace pretends to have been inspired by Bacchus in order to rhapsodize on the name and fame of Caesar. The theme here may possibly be the overthrow of Cleopatra, or more probably the bestowal of the title of Augustus upon Octavian.

[2] A bacchante; a priestess of Bacchus, or one reveling in the worship of Bacchus.

[3] A river in Thrace.

[4] A mountain in Thrace.

[5] God of the wine press.

[6] Metre: Second Asclepiadean.

III, 26

Till late I lived a favorite with the girls,
And not without some glory my battles waged;
    But now this wall will hold my armor,
        It and my lute with its service finished,

This wall which guards the left side of Venus, her
The sea-born one. Here, here put the blazing lights,
    The torches, crowbars, and the bow which
        Threatened the doors that were shut against me.[1]

O goddess, you who dwell in blest Cyprus and
Hold Memphis, too, both free from Sithonian[2] snow,
    O queen, with your uplifted lash, touch
        Once that disdainful, that haughty Chloe![3]

[1] This utterly charming lament in which Horace dedicates to Venus his useless arms, the lover's lute, the torch that lights him to his lady's door—only to be denied admission—is one of the reasons why, after two thousand years, the Odes of Horace still lend their light and color to the hearts of men.
[2] Thracian.
[3] Metre: Alcaic Strophe.

Let[1] the screeching owl's ill-foreboding omen,
Pregnant bitch, the yellow-gray wolf from Lanu-
vinian fields descending, and mother vixen
    Go with the wicked;

And if, darting slantwise across the path, a
Serpent like an arrow shall terrify the
Ponies, let it break off the journey; as shrewd
    Seer for whoever's

Sake I fear, I'll summon the croaking raven
With my prayer from out of the East before the
Bird again revisits the stagnant marshes,
    Foretelling showers.

But may you be happy where'er you choose, and
Live remembering me, Galatea; neither
Let the luckless magpie nor vagrant crow pro-
    hibit your going.

Yet do you see how setting Orion rushes
On in tumult? Well do I know how black may
Be the gulf of Adria, how deceitful
    Iapyx,[2] the lucky.

May the wives and sons of the foe know also,
Feel the blinding fury of Auster[3] rising,
Roar of darkling sea and the shore line trembling
    Under its lashing.

Thus Europa[4] trusted her snowy body
To the crafty bull, and though once undaunted,
Paled at billows teeming with monsters and the
    Perils around her:

She who late in meadows was fond of flowers,
And for nymphs was maker of tribute garlands;
Now through gleaming darkness saw only stars and
    Heaving of waters.

Soon as she reached Crete with its hundred cities
Strong, she cried, "O father! O daughter's name I
Left behind, O daughter's affection which was
    Conquered by passion!

When and whither now have I come? One death is
Light for this maid's trespass. Am I awake as
I deplore my shameful offense? Or does a
    Vain vision mock me

Guiltless, flying in through the ivory gate with
But a dream? Oh, which was the better? Was it
Riding through the lengthening billows, or to
    Gather fresh flowers?

Oh, if anyone in my wrath will give me
Now that cursed bull, I shall try to wound him
With the sword, and break off the horns of that once
    Greatly loved monster.

Shameless have I gone from my father's gods, and
Shameless now I tarry while Death is waiting.
Gods who hear me! would that among the lions
    Naked I wander!

Ere some base disease thin my comely cheeks, and
Ere the sap depart from the tender prey, I
Long, I seek, while still I am fair, to furnish
    Food for the tigers.

Still my absent father, reproaching, urges:
'Vile Europa, why do you wait to die? For
From this mountain ash with your handy girdle,
    You could be hanging!

Or if cliffs and rocks sharp for death may please you
Better—come then, give the swift wind your body;
Come, unless you'd rather perform the spinning
    Set by some mistress,

And as concubine, though of royal blood, to
Some barbaric queen be delivered.'" As she
Wailed, false-smiling Venus stood near her, and her
    Son with his bow slack.

Soon, when she had mocked her enough, "Refrain," she
Said, "from wrath and heated reproaches, since the
Hated bull will give you his horns again, that
    Now you may rend them.

You know not that you are the bride of Jove, the
Undefeated! Cease sobbing; learn to bear great
Fortune rightly; yours is the name that half the
    World soon shall carry."[5]

---

[1] The legend of Europa. Horace seems to begin by saying, "Let there be bad
omens for the bad; but let all good omens go with you, Galatea (a fictitious
name), since go you must. Live happily, but forget me not. I know the terrors of
the wintry Adriatic Sea; let the wives and children of our foes tremble at them,
even as Europa trembled." With this, he passes to his real theme, the rape of

Europa and her self-reproachful soliloquy when she is far from home, and at the end the explanation and consolation of Venus.

² See I, 3. Evidently Galatea's itinerary was along the Appian Way to Brundisium, thence across to Greece.

³ The hot, dry, south wind.

⁴ The daughter of Agenor, king of Phoenicia. Jupiter, under the form of a bull, carried her off to Crete. The continent of Europe was named after her.

⁵ Metre: Sapphic Strophe.

What[1] could I better do on this,
　　Neptune's festival day? Quickly bring forth the wine,
Lyda,[2] Caecuban wine long stored;
　　Storm the fort of your sound, well-advised principles!
You know noon is declining, yet—
　　Just as if flying day lingered!—you balk to snatch
From the storeroom that unused jar
　　Waiting there ever since Bibulus'[3] consulship.
We shall sing, you and I, by turns
　　Of Neptune, of the green locks of the Nereid nymphs;[4]
You shall sing with your curving lyre
　　Of Latona and fleet Cynthia's javelins:
At the end we'll praise her who holds
　　Cnidos,[5] governs the bright, glittering Cyclades,
Visits Paphos,[6] by yoked swans drawn:[7]
　　Night shall also be sung, praised in a worthy hymn.[8]

---

[1] A summons to Lyda to celebrate the festival of Neptune, not in the company of a picnicking crowd, but with good old Caecuban wine and a song at home.

[2] Whether Lyda is the stern housekeeper at the Sabine farm or a casual flute girl is not made clear, but the former supposition seems more probable.

[3] The sluggish consul with Julius Caesar in 59 B.C., when the wits dated their letters *Iulio et Caesare consulibus.* The name Bibulus is ominous, meaning "drinking freely."

[4] Sea goddesses wear the hues of "the pale-green sea-groves" (Alfred, Lord Tennyson, "The Merman").

[5] See I, 30.

[6] A city on the island of Cyprus, sacred to Venus, with a celebrated temple to her.

[7] Cf. Edmund Spenser, *Prothalamion*, l. 63: "that same pair (of swans) Which through the sky draw Venus' silver team."

[8] Metre: Second Asclepiadean.

For you, Maecenas,[1] scion of Tuscan kings,
A mellow wine in cask never broached as yet,
  Some rosy blooms and, for your hair, the
    Fragrant Arabian balm-nut essence

Have long been waiting here: tear yourself away,
Nor gaze on Tibur's marshes forevermore,
  The sloping fields of Aefula,[2] the
    Heights of Telegonus, father-slayer.[3]

Forsake the wealth that cloys, and your palace set
To reach toward lofty clouds; cease to contemplate,
  To marvel at the smoke, the noise, the
    Grandeur of prosperous Rome's abundance.

Sometimes a change is pleasing to wealthy men,
And suppers, neatly served 'neath a humble roof
  Without the purple tapestries, have
    Smoothed out the lines from a careworn forehead.

Already now Andromeda's brilliant sire[4]
Shows forth his hidden flame, and now Procyon[5]
  And savage Leo's[6] stars are raging,
    Now that the sun has brought back the dry days.

Already now the shepherd, grown weary, seeks
The shade-trees and the stream with his languid flock,
  And rough Silvanus'[7] thickets; quiet
    Banks of the stream miss the straying breezes.

You are concerned what policy fits the state,
And, troubled still, you fear for the city: what
    The Seres[8] plot, and Bactra[9] ruled by
        Cyrus, and Tanais[10] that seat of discord.

A prudent God encloses the future's end
In misty night, and smiles if a mortal frets
    With more than rightful fear. Remember
        Calmly to set what is here in order;

The rest is swept along like the river's course,
Which sometimes glides along to the Tuscan Sea[11]
    In peace, mid-channel; sometimes whirling
        Smoothly worn pebbles, uprooted tree trunks,

And flocks and houses, churning them all in one
'Midst roar of hills and clamor of near-by groves
    When fierce, destructive flood and savage
        Deluge enrages its quiet flowing.

That man lives happy, lord of himself, who is
From day to day allowed to declare, "I've lived:
    Tomorrow let the Father spread the
        Heavens with dark cloud or purest sunlight;

He nonetheless will never make void that which
Is past, nor will he ever recast the mold,
    Nor make undone, nor will he alter
        That which the vanishing hour has brought me."

A willful goddess, Fortune, she takes delight
In cruelty, in playing a mocking game,
    And shifts her fickle favors, being
        Now kind to me, now another gracing.

171

I praise her while she stays; if she stirs swift wings,
I give back all she gave me, and in my worth,
My virtue, wrap myself, and seek out
Poverty, excellent though undowered.

'Tis not my way, though mast groan beneath the storms
Of Africus, to fall into abject prayers,
By vows to bargain that my wares of
Cyprus and Tyre may not add their riches

To greedy waters: then in my two-oared skiff's
Protection, gentle breezes shall bear me safe
Through tumult of Aegean waters—
Soft breezes, Pollux, and his twin brother.[12]

---

[1] An invitation to Maecenas to visit Horace at the Sabine farm. Lines 25–28 seem to indicate Augustus' absence in the West, 25 and 26 B.C.

[2] Aefula (sometimes spelled Aesula), a town near Tibur.

[3] Tusculum; a town of Latium (now Frascati), founded by Telegonus, son of Circe and Ulysses, who traveled in search of his father and unwittingly killed him in Ithaca.

[4] Cepheus, king of Ethiopia, the father of Andromeda, was said to have become a constellation near the Little Bear. It begins early in July to show forth the bright light which before was hidden.

[5] Procyon: the minor Dog Star, which rises in the morning, July 15, about eleven days before Sirius, the "dog of Orion."

[6] The constellation Leo.

[7] The god of woods and all places planted with trees.

[8] The Chinese.

[9] A Greek Bactrian kingdom existed about 250–125 B.C.

[10] Tanais: the river Don, in Russia.

[11] That part of the Mediterranean between Italy and Corsica and Sardinia.

[12] Metre: Alcaic Strophe.

III, 30

More enduring than bronze I've built my monument[1]
Overtopping the royal pile of the pyramids,
Which no ravenous rain, neither Aquilo's rage
Shall suffice to destroy, nor the unnumbered years
As they pass one by one, nor shall the flight of time.
I shall not wholly die; no, a great part of me
Shall escape from death's Queen;[2] still shall my fame rise fresh
In posterity's praise, while to the Capitol
Still the high priest and mute maiden ascend the Hill.[3]
From where Aufidus[4] brawls and from that thirsty land
In which Daunus[5] once ruled over his rustic tribes,
I, grown great though born low,[6] I shall be named as first[7]
To have spun Grecian song into Italian strands
With their lyrical modes. Take this proud eminence
Won by your just deserts; and with the Delphic bay,
O Melpomene, now graciously bind my hair.[8]

---

[1] This famous ode is the epilogue to the first three books of the odes, which were published in 23 B.C. In it Horace prophesies his immortality. It is the proud consciousness of a humble man that his work will endure.

[2] Deaths were registered in the temple of Libitina.

[3] The Capitoline Hill, on which stood the Capitol, the symbol of the eternity of Rome.

[4] A river of Apulia, swift and violent; now the Ofanto.

[5] A mythic king of a part of Apulia.

[6] Horace anticipates sneers at his humble origin.

[7] Horace's proud claim to originality is that he first introduced the Greek lyric metres into Latin literature. Catullus had made a few experimental attempts, but Horace ignores these.

[8] Metre: First Asclepiadean.

BOOK IV

"Last of my loves." — IV, 11

Venus, after so long a truce
    Do you now move to war? Spare me, I pray, I pray![1]
I am not the same man I was
    In sweet Cinara's[2] reign. Cease to persuade me now,
Cruel mother of tender loves,
    Who at fifty am grown flint to your soft commands,
Stop prevailing on me: be gone
    Where the prayers of young men coaxingly call you back.
How much better to visit then
    Paullus Maximus'[3] house; winged by your dazzling swans
You shall hie there in revelry
    If you seek for an apt, suitable heart to fire.
He is noble and handsome both,
    In behalf of disturbed plaintiffs he is not mute;
He, a youth of a hundred skills,
    He will bear far and wide all your bright flags of war.
When, triumphant, he shall have laughed
    At his rival's rich gifts given with lavish hand,
He will place you in marble there
    'Neath a cedar-beam roof close to the Alban Lakes.
Through your nostrils you shall inhale
    Clouds of incense and myrrh; there you will be regaled
By the strains of the lyre and by
    Berecynthian[4] flute blended with piping reeds;
In your shrine there twice every day
    Boys and delicate girls praising your sacred name
Thrice will stamp with the snow-white foot
    On the ground in the mode Salian dancers[5] use.
Woman gladdens me now no more,

Nor does boy, nor the fond hope of a kindred mind;
Nor care I to compete in wine,
Nor with garlands of fresh flowers to bind my brows.
But then why, Ligurinus,[6] why
Does a hesitant tear now trickle down my cheeks:
Why, alas, do the facile words
Fall so awkwardly still, falter in midst of speech?
Now again in my nightly dreams
I am holding you caught; now I run after you
Fleeing over the Martian Field;[7]
Through the swift-rolling streams, hard heart, I follow you![8]

---

[1] At the age of fifty, Horace collected into this fourth book of the odes an aftermath of occasional poems, including several great patriotic odes written at the direct request of Augustus to commemorate the victories of his stepsons and to perpetuate the eternal glory of Rome. Horace opens the book by gracefully reminding the reader that he is no longer to be regarded as the light singer of loves.

This exquisite first ode is one of the tenderest and most moving in all literature. Horace says he is too old for love, and begs Venus to spare him.

[2] Cinara was apparently the only flesh-and-blood woman of all Horace's Lydias, Glyceras, and Chloes.

[3] Paulus Fabius Maximus, consul in 11 B.C., was a friend of Ovid and of Augustus.

[4] See note to I, 18.

[5] See notes to I, 36 and 37.

[6] An imaginary person.

[7] A grassy plain along the river Tiber, and dedicated to Mars; used for games and recreation.

[8] Metre: Second Asclepiadean.

Whoso strives to emulate Pindar,[1] Jullus,[2]
Mounts on wings wax-joined by Daedalian art,[3] and
To some glassy sea he will give his name, his
    Name but to water.

Like a torrent rushing from mountain height, which
Storms have swollen past its accustomed banks, he
Sweeps and surges, boundless in deep-mouthed measures,
    Pindar the mighty.

Worthy to be given Apollo's laurel,
Whether in bold dithyrambs he unrolls new
Phrases, and is carried along on verse from
    Law all unloosened,

Whether he may sing of the gods or kings, the
Offspring of the gods, through whom Centaurs[4] fell in
Well-earned death, and quenched fell the flaming of the
    Dreaded Chimaera,

Or of those exalted ones whom the palm of
Elis leads back home, or should cite a boxer
Or a horse—and give them a better gift than
    Hundreds of statues—

Or laments some youth torn from weeping bride, and
Raises to the heavens his strength and courage,
Lauds his golden morals, and rescues him from
    Sable-clad Orcus.[5]

Mighty winds lift up the Dircaean swan[6] as
Oft, Antonius, as he soars to lofty
Realms of clouds. But I, like a Matine[7] bee in
    Manner of working,

I, of lesser talent with greater toil, near
Tibur's marshy banks and moist groves, I gather
Grateful thyme, and carefully fashion thus my
    Painstaking verses.

You shall sing, a poet with louder plectrum,
Sing of Caesar, handsome with well-earned garland,
When he leads the warlike Sygambri up our
    Own sacred hillside.[8]

Never gave the Fates and the kindly gods a
Greater, better gift to the world than he, nor
Shall give, even though to the former age of
    Gold time turns backward.

You shall sing of days of rejoicing and the
City's public sport and the Forum freed from
Strife by his return, the vouchsafed return of
    Valiant Augustus.

Then a goodly part of my voice shall join, if
What I say be worthy of hearing; happy
Shall I sing, "O day to be praised! Fair day!" with
    Caesar returned home.

As you move along, we shall sing "Ho! Triumph!"
Not just once, we, citizens all, "Ho! Triumph!"
Then shall sing, and give to the kindly gods our
    Offerings of incense.

From your vows ten bulls and as many cows will
Bring release; for me shall a tender calf just
Weaned, which now grows up in abundant grasses,
    Furnish my offering.

With his horns he patterns the moon's curved fires
When she comes again on her third night's rising;
Where he bears a mark, he is white to view, the
    Rest is all tawny.[9]

[1] A celebrated lyric poet of Thebes, contemporary with Aeschylus.

[2] Jullus Antonius, the son of the triumvir and Fulvia, was brought up by his stepmother Octavia and treated as a member of the Julian house by Augustus. This ode was apparently composed about 14 B.C. in anticipation of Augustus' return from the West, where he had gone in 16 B.C. after the defeat of M. Lollius by the Sygambrians. Jullus Antonius may have suggested that Horace should celebrate the achievements of the Emperor in Pindaric strain.

[3] Daedalus: an Athenian, father of Icarus, and builder of the Cretan labyrinth. In order to escape from Crete he made wax wings for himself and his son Icarus. Icarus flew too near the sun, the wax melted, and he fell into the Aegean Sea.

[4] See note to I, 18.

[5] The god of the infernal regions.

[6] Dirce was a fountain northwest of Thebes in Boeotia. Horace is referring here to Pindar as the "Theban swan."

[7] Matinus: a mountain in Apulia, not far from Horace's birthplace.

[8] As prisoners, that is. The Sygambrians had defeated the legate Lollius, but hastened to make peace with Augustus.

[9] Metre: Sapphic Strophe.

On whose birth, O Melpomene,[1]
    You looked once and for all, glancing with kindly eye,
Him no Isthmian[2] toil will mold
    To a boxer of fame, neither shall tireless steed
Draw him onward triumphant in
    Grecian chariot race, nor shall his deeds of war
Make him known to the Capitol
    As the leader who crushed kings' haughty threats, nor shall
Show him crowned with the Delian leaves;[3]
    But the streams that flow past Tibur of fertile field,
Thick-grown tresses of leafy groves:
    These shall make him a name famous in Grecian song.
So it is that the sons of Rome—
    Her, the chiefest of all cities—have deigned to rank
Me among the poetic choir,
    And I'm now bitten less fiercely by envy's tooth.
You who govern the dulcet noise
    Of the golden-toned shell, Muse of Pieria,[4]
Who could give the mute fishes song—
    Yes, the song of the swan!—if you were so disposed,
All of this is your grace toward me
    That I'm now pointed out bard of the Roman lyre
By the finger of passers-by:
    That I breathe, that I please (if I do please) is yours![5]

---

[1] The Muse of poetry.

[2] The Isthmus of Corinth, where the Isthmian Games were celebrated every five years. The victors received a pine garland.

[3] Of Apollo. The Delian leaves were laurel.

[4] The Muses are frequently called the Pierides, from Pieria, a region of Macedonia connected with their cult.

[5] Metre: Second Asclepiadean.

IV, 4

Just[1] like the winged priest of the thunderbolt,
Whom Jupiter, the king of the gods, gave power
    O'er roaming birds, because he had on
        Golden-haired Ganymede[2] proved him faithful,

Once youth and native vigor have driven him,
Unused to hardships, out of the nest, whom soon
    Though timorous the winds of spring have
        Shown how to make unaccustomed efforts,

Since winter's storms are gone; whom, as enemy,
An eager swoop soon sent on the sheepfold, now
    Upon some struggling serpents has the
        Love of a feast and a battle plunged him;

Or like some lion recently weaned from milk
And breast of tawny dam, whom a kid intent
    On pleasant pastures spied, by whose new
        Teeth she could see she was doomed to perish;

Beneath the Rhaetic Alps, the Vindelici
Likewise beheld our Drusus there waging war;
    (The source from whence the custom comes of
        Arming their hands with the battle-axes

Of Amazons, I have not inquired—it is
Not well to know all things!); but their conqu'ring hosts
    So long victorious far and wide, now
        Conquered in turn by his youthful planning,

Have learned what intellect and ability
Can do when duly nurtured in heav'n-blest homes,
    And what Augustus' love paternal
        Now has achieved for the youthful Neros.

Brave sons are born from those who are brave and good;
In bullocks and in steeds is their sires' strength,
    And neither do the bold, fierce eagles
        Procreate peaceful and timid pigeons.

And yet instruction quickens the inbred power,
And proper training fortifies character;
    When once morality has failed, then
        Faults soon corrupt what was good by nature.

The debt you owe, O Rome, to great Nero's race[3]
Then let the stream Metaurus its witness bear,
    And conquered Hasdrubal, and that fair
        Day when the shadows all fled from Latium;

That day which first with genial vict'ry smiled
Since, like a flame through pines, the dread African
    Through towns of Italy had charged, or
        Eurus when riding Sicilian billows.

From that time forth, by ever-propitious toil
Young men of Rome increased in their strength, and shrines
    Laid waste by wicked Punic onslaught
        Now once again held their gods set upright.

At length exclaimed perfidious Hannibal:
"Weak deer, the prey of ravening wolves, we still
    Pursue them, whom to trick and hide from,
        Whom to escape is abundant triumph.

That dauntless race, from Ilium's[4] ashes sprung,
Which tossed on Tuscan seas, bore its shrines, its sons,
    Its aged sires, and carried them to
        Italy's towns, to Ausonian cities,[5]

Just as an ilex, shorn by rough, two-edged ax
On Algidus where thick grow the dusky leaves,
    Through injuries, through mutilation,
        Draws from the steel itself strength and spirit.

Not more persistently did the Hydra,[6] lopped
In body, grow more strong against Hercules,
    Who grieved to lose; not Colchian soil nor
        Echion's[7] Thebes bore a stranger portent.

You plunge it deep, it comes forth the fairer still;
Contend, and with much glory it will subdue
    Its conqueror till now victorious,
        And will wage wars for our wives to tell of.

Proud messengers to Carthage I'll send no more:
For fallen, fallen now is our hope, all crushed,
    The fortune of our name is perished
        Now that our Hasdrubal has been slaughtered."

For there is nothing Claudian hands cannot
Achieve, which Jupiter with his gracious nod
    Protects; and thus it is that cautious
        Wisdom will guide them through war's sharp trials.[8]

---

[1] This ode in particular, as well as the fourth book in general, was written, Suetonius tells us, at the emperor's express command. It celebrates the victories of Drusus, the emperor's younger stepson and his favorite, over certain of the unruly Alpine tribes: the Videlicians, the Rhaetians, the Brenni, and the Genauni. Drusus then probably turned westward to join his brother Tiberius (afterward

emperor). Shorey (*Horace—Odes and Epodes*, 426) tells us that "Tiberius penetrated the gorges of the Upper Rhine and Inn in every direction; and at the conclusion of a brilliant and rapid campaign, the two brothers had effected the complete subjugation of the country of the Grisons and the Tyrol, which with adjacent territory constituted the province of Rhaetia."

Horace often professes that he is unable to sing of war, and in this instance he evades the difficulty by a Pindaric treatment with a long historical digression in lines 37–73. He begins the ode by comparing Drusus to a new-fledged eagle swooping down on its quarry, or to a fresh-weaned lion rending its first victim.

[2] Ganymede: a son of Laomedon, who, on account of his youthful beauty, was carried off by Jupiter's eagle from Mount Ida to heaven, and there made Jupiter's cupbearer in place of Hebe.

[3] From here on, Horace sings the praises of the young princes by recalling the famous exploits of their ancestor, C. Claudius Nero, whose courage and valor were mainly responsible for the defeat of Hasdrubal at the river Metaurus in the Second Punic War, 207 B.C.

[4] Ilium: Troy.

[5] The Ausones: a very ancient, perhaps Greek, name of the inhabitants of middle and lower Italy.

[6] A Hydra with fifty heads that keeps watch at the gates of the lower world.

[7] Echion: one of the heroes who sprang up from the dragon's teeth sown by Cadmus.

[8] Metre: Alcaic Strophe.

Guard[1] of Romulus' race, born when the gods were kind,
O most excellent guard, absent now far too long;
Having promised the grave Council of Fathers a
    Quick returning—oh, then return!

Give your country your light, give it again, great chief:
For when, springlike, your face shines on the populace,
Then the day seems more fair, time passes pleasantly,
    And the sun shines more brightly still.

As a mother with prayers calls for her youthful son
Whom the South Wind by blasts keeps from his pleasant home,
By his envious blasts o'er the Carpathian Sea,
    Keeps for more than a year from home,

Calls by vows and by prayers, omens and solemn signs,
Nor her face turns away yet from the curving shore;
So our fatherland yearns, stabbed by her loyal need,
    Yearns for Caesar, our Caesar still.

For in safety the ox roams through the countryside,
Ceres nurtures the fields, she and kind Faustitas;[2]
Safe the mariners speed over the tranquil sea,
    Honor shrinks from the breath of blame.

By no lusts is the pure household polluted here;
Law and morals have now vanquished the taint of vice;
Praised are wives bearing sons like to their sires; as a
    Comrade, punishment follows crime.

Who dreads Parthians now, who the chilled Scythian,
Who the brood which that fierce Germany still spawns forth,
While our Caesar is safe? Who'd waste a care about
   War with savage Iberia?

Each man passes the day here on his hills of home,
And twines tendrils of vine onto the widowed trees,
Gladly turns in to sup, and at the second course
   He invokes you as deity.

For to you with much prayer pays he his homage, and
With wine poured from the bowls mingles your name divine
With the Lares[3]—like Greece, mindful of Castor and
   Of her mighty one, Hercules.

"O long holidays then grant to us, worthy chief,
Guarding Italy's peace!" Sober, we say at morn
When the day is still whole; say it when flushed with wine
   As the sun sinks beneath the sea.[4]

---

1 This ode, following the one in praise of Drusus, celebrates Augustus as the
restorer of peace. Following the defeat of Lollius by the Sygambrians in 16 B.C.,
Augustus spent three years in the West in order to restore order in Gaul and
Spain. This is a carefully polished ode in his honor, imploring his return to
Rome.
   2 Goddess of the fertility of the soil.
   3 The *lares* were the household gods. Their images were placed either in a
little shrine by the hearth, or in a small chapel in the interior of the house.
   4 Metre: Third Asclepiadean.

IV, 6

God,[1] the punisher of a boastful tongue, whom
Tityos and Niobe's children knew, and
He—almost the victor of lofty Troy—the
    Phthian Achilles,[2]

Greater than the rest, yet no match for you as
Warrior, though the son of the sea-born Thetis,
He with dreadful spear shook the Trojan towers, for
    He was a fighter.

Like some pine tree struck by the biting steel, or
Like some cypress trunk overthrown by Eurus,[3]
Stretched full length he fell, and he laid his neck in
    Troy's dusty ruins.

Not within the horse (as Minerva's gift false
Feigned) would he have slyly deceived the festive
Trojans, and surprised them in Priam's palace,
    Gay with their dancing;

But toward captives openly harsh—alas, such
Crime, alas!—for he would have burned in Greek fire
Lisping children, even those hid within the
    Womb of the mother,

Had not then the Father of Gods, won over
By your prayers and those of the gentle Venus,
Promised to Aeneas walls built beneath a
    Kindlier omen.

Teacher of the lyre to the Grecian Thalia,
You who bathe your locks in the stream of Xanthus,[4]
Phoebus, guard the honor of Daunia's Muse, O
    Unshorn Agyieus.[5]

Phoebus gave me art and my inspiration,
Phoebus skill of song and the name of poet,
You, O noble virgins, you boys, you young men,
    Sprung from famed fathers,

Wards of Delos' goddess,[6] who with her bowstring
Stays the deer in flight and the fleeing lynxes,
Keep your time to Lesbian measures and the
    Beat of my thumbing.

Duly now the son of Latona singing,
Duly sing the lamp of the night that rises
Brightly, prospers harvests, and speeds the leaning
    Months to roll forward.

When a bride you'll say: "I have sung a song which
Pleased the gods, at Secular Holiday I
Sang the song, instructed in measured strains of
    Horace, the poet."[7]

---

[1] A prelude addressed to the chorus of noble youths and maidens who were to
sing the Carmen Saeculare. (See preface, above.)
    Shorey's (Horace—Odes and Epodes, 437) explanatory comment on this ode
is as follows: "Apollo that didst punish Niobe and Tityos and overthrow even
Achilles, who else would have left alive no child of Troy to found Rome under
happier auspices, thou inspirer of the Grecian muse, uphold today the honor of
Latin song. And you, noble maids, mark well the measure of this sacred chant.
Happy matrons, one day you will boast that on the great festival day you learned
and sang the strains of Horace the Bard."

[2] Apollo slew Achilles, and so made possible the escape of Aeneas and the
founding of Rome. Phthia (or Phthiotis) was the birthplace of Achilles.

[3] The southeast wind.
[4] A river of Troy.
[5] An epithet of Apollo.
[6] Diana.
[7] Metre: Sapphic Strophe.

Now are the snows all fled,[1] and the grass returns to the fields,
    Tresses return to trees;
Earth to her annual changes, her beautiful changes yields;
    The bed of the river receives
The chastened floods. The nymphs and their sisters with naked grace
    Dare lead the dance of spring.
Nothing immortal: so warns the year and kindly day
    Which time is ravishing.
Frosts melt, and hard on the heels of Spring will Summer tread,
    Which soon, too soon, must die.
Autumn will all of her lavish and fruit-laden bounty spread
    Where soon dull Winter will lie.
Moons will swiftly return and repair the heaven's loss;
    But we, when we shall descend
Whither descended our father Aeneas,[2] rich Tullus and Ancus,[3]
    In dust and in shadow shall end.
Who knows, or ever can know, if to the last today
    The gods will add tomorrow?
Give to your friendly soul your wealth, and far away
    Your heirs will flee in sorrow.
When once for all you shall die and sadly go downward hence
    To Minos'[4] august decree,
Not, Torquatus,[5] your birth, your love, nor your eloquence
    Shall ever set you free.
Even Diana from Hades never could liberate
    The chaste Hippolytus;[6]
Nor could brave Theseus the chains of Lethe break
    From his dear[7] Pirithoüs.[8]

¹ In this poetically beautiful, but profoundly melancholy, ode Horace notes the changes of the seasons, which come and go and come again; but man, when he departs, ends in dust and shadow.

² Vergil's *Aeneid* had recently been published. Aeneas, the son of Venus and Anchises, had escaped from burning Troy, made his way westward to Italy after years of wanderings, and become the ancestor of the Romans. He was worshipped after death as Jupiter Indiges.

³ Livy wrote of the glory and wealth of King Tullus. Ancus is given as an example of a good man.

⁴ A judge in the infernal regions.

⁵ Torquatus was a lawyer and a friend of Horace.

⁶ Hippolytus was the son of Theseus. His death was caused by the fury of a woman scorned—his stepmother Phaedra, who, when repulsed, denounced him to his father. During his lifetime he had been devoted to the service of the goddess Diana.

⁷ Pirithoüs was the son of Ixion, king of the Lapithae. After the death of his wife, Hippodamia, he descended with his friend Theseus to the infernal regions to carry away Proserpina; but they were seized and put into chains. Theseus was later rescued by Hercules, who vainly endeavored to save Pirithoüs also.

⁸ Metre: a loose approximation of the 1st Archilochian; done as an experiment, using end-rhyme.

I would give to my friends goblets of cherished bronze,[1]
Censorinus,[2] would give willingly bowls of brass,
Would my tripods bestow, prizes of valiant Greeks;
Nor would you bear away less than the best of gifts,
If in truth I were rich, rich in those works of art
Which Parrhasius[3] limned, or those which Scopas carved,
This one working in stone, that one in liquid hues,
Skilled to show now a man, now to present a god.
But this power is not mine; nor does your fortune lack,
Or your temperament need, flatteries such as these.
You take pleasure in songs; songs we can give to you,
And the worth of the gift we can proceed to tell:
For not statues engraved, cut at the state's expense,
Whereby life's breath returns, flows through great chiefs again
Even after their death; Hannibal's hurried flights
Nor his threats which were hurled back in his very teeth,
Nor the flames of that cursed Carthage, not one of them
Does more clearly proclaim praises of him who from
Conquered Africa came with a proud title won
Than Pierides can, Muses Calabrian;
Nor, if annals are mute, will you receive reward
For those things you did well. What would we know of him
(Mars' and Ilia's son) had jealous silence stood
As opposed to the great merits of Romulus?
Virtue, public acclaim, tongues of great poets thus
Have made Aeacus[4] safe, snatched from the Stygian waves,
Have immortalized him, set in the splendid isles.
That man worthy of praise will not the Muse let die,
But in heaven enshrines. Still tireless Hercules

Thus is present at feasts yearned for—the feasts of Jove;
Thus Tyndareus' sons,[5] bright-shining stars of light,
Snatch from depths of the sea shattered and broken barks.
Bacchus, now with green vines having adorned his brows,
To propitious events guides our devoted prayers.[6]

---

[1] Probably as presents on the occasion of the Saturnalia.

[2] C. Marcius Censorinus, consul in 8 B.C., is known only by this ode—which thus fulfills its promise—and by a mention of him by Velleius.

[3] The great painter of the close of the fifth century B.C. Scopas was the great sculptor of the first half of the fourth century.

[4] Aeacus: son of Jupiter and Europa. On account of his justice, he was made a judge in the lower world.

[5] The twin stars Castor and Pollux.

[6] Metre: First Asclepiadean.

Lest you believe perchance that these words will die,
I, who was born near far-sounding Aufidus,
    I speak by arts not known before now
        Words to be linked to the lyre's sweet music:

Although first place Maeonian Homer[1] holds,
The Muse of Pindar, yes, and the Cean Muse
    Are not unknown, Alcaeus' threatenings,
        Neither Stesichorus' stately verses;

Nor that which once Anacreon sang in sport
Has time erased; the love of Aeolia's maid[2]
    Still breathes, and still her passions live which
        Were to the strings of her lyre confided.

Not only did Laconian[3] Helen burn,
Seeing the shining locks of some profligate,
    Admire his gold-embroidered garments,
        Struck by his splendor, his regal comrades;

Nor was bold Teucer[4] first with the Cretan bow
To aim his arrows straight; and not only once
    Was Troy besieged, and not alone did
        Sthenelus and huge Idomeneus fight

Great battles worth the song of the Muses; nor
Was fiery Hector first to sustain rough blows,
    Nor yet the keen Deiphobus for
        Sake of their virtuous wives and children.

Brave men have lived before Agamemnon—yes,
And many!—but, unwept and unknown, they all
    Are closed within a long, dark night, for
        They were without an inspired poet.

Hid virtue differs little from buried sloth.
I'll not keep silent, Lollius,[5] nor unpraised
    Upon my pages leave you, neither
        Suffer oblivion, pale, unpunished,

To seize upon your struggles, your many works.
A prudent soul is yours, and a steadfast mind
    Foreseeing many matters, both in
        Prosperous times and in times of peril.

A punisher of covetous fraud are you,
You spurn the gold that draws to itself all things;
    A consul not for one year only,
        But just as oft as a good and faithful

Judge placed his honor over advantage, and
With noble mien the bribes of the guilty scorned,
    So with victorious display, he
        Carried his arms through opposing forces.

Not him with great possessions should you in truth
Call blest; with better right does he claim the name
    Of happy man who realizes
        How to make use of the gods' gifts wisely,

Is skilled to meet harsh poverty and endure,
As one who dreads dishonor far more than death;
A man like that for friends beloved,
    Or for his country fears not to perish.[6]

[1] Horace names Homer and a succession of Greek poets.
[2] Sappho, the great poetess of Lesbos.
[3] Spartan.
[4] Horace enumerates heroes of the Trojan War.
[5] This ode was written in praise of M. Lollius, a trusted minister of Augustus. He was consul in 21 B.C., and governor of Gaul, where he was defeated by the Sygambrians in 16 B.C. He died in the East in 1 B.C., while acting as the tutor and advisor of Augustus' grandson, Gaius Caesar. Velleius accused Lollius of greed and hypocrisy, but Horace springs to his friend's defense.
[6] Metre: Alcaic Strophe.

O still cruel,[1] yes, still! potent with gifts Venus has given you,
When at last to your pride, sudden, the first down of your beard shall come,
And those ringlets which now flow down your back finally shall be shorn,[2]
And the flush of your cheek, color which now outvies the Punic rose,
Ligurinus, your face, changed in its looks, bristled and rough shall be;
Mirrorwise you will look, saying "Alas!" seeing your altered self,
"Today judgment is there; why was it not while I was yet a boy?
Or, since knowledge has come, where are the fresh, unwrinkled cheeks
    of youth?"[3]

[1] To the beautiful youth Ligurinus (IV, 1).
[2] A Roman boy's long hair was usually cut when he assumed the *toga virilis*, the dress of manhood.
[3] Metre: Fifth Asclepiadean.

Alban wine, a caskful, I have here, Phyllis,[1]
Past its ninth year now; and within my garden
Parsley growing, parsley for twining garlands,
 Plenty of ivy,

Wherewith, having bound up your hair, you glisten;
Smiling bright with silver, my house; the altar,
Decked with sacred boughs, with a slain lamb's blood now
 Longs to be sprinkled;

All the household band hastens hither, thither,
Girls are rushing, mingled with speeding slave boys;
Flames are flicking upward and whirling sooty
 Smoke into eddies.

Yet, that you may know to what merrymaking
You are bidden—it is to celebrate fair
April's ides, the day which divides the month of
 Venus, the sea-born.

Rightly festive, almost to me more sacred
Than my own birthday, is this day from whose dawn
My Maecenas reckons his gliding years, his
 Rich-flowing seasons.

Telephus, the youth whom you seek, is not of
Your degree; a wealthy and wanton girl has
Taken him in thrall, and she holds him captive,
 Bound with sweet fetters.

Phaëthon,[2] consumed by the flame, is warning
'Gainst ambitious hopes; winged Pegasus,[3] who
Spurned an earthborn rider, Bellerophon, gives
    Weighty example

Always to pursue that which best befits you;
Deeming it as wicked to hope beyond the
Lawful, shun one not of your own condition.
    Last of my loves (for

Never shall I burn for another woman
After this!): Come now, learn these measures which your
Lovely voice will render; black cares will grow the
    Less[4] with your singing.[5]

[1] An invitation to Phyllis to come and help celebrate Maecenas' birthday. Maecenas was out of favor at court during the last years of his life, and this is the only mention of him in this book devoted especially to Augustus.

[2] The son of Helios and Clymene, who, attempting to drive the chariot of his father, the sun, set the world on fire, and was killed by a thunderbolt of Jupiter.

[3] The winged horse which sprang from the blood of Medusa, and produced the fountain Hippocrene by a blow from his hoof. He threw off his lord Bellerophon, when he tried to ride into the heavenly habitations and mix with the company of Zeus.

[4] This exquisite end is one more evidence of the enduring charm of Horace.

[5] Metre: Sapphic Strophe.

Now the comrades of spring, breezes which calm the sea,
Tranquil currents from Thrace, push out and swell the sails;
Now the fields are not stiff, nor do the rivers roar,
    Being swollen with winter's snow.

She is building her nest, mourning (unhappy bird!)
Itys[1] piteously, she the Cecropian[2]
Line's eternal reproach, seeing how wickedly
    She once punished the kings' brute lusts.

They that tend the fat sheep sing in the fresh, new grass,
Sing their songs to the pipe, and they delight the god
To whom flocks and the dark hills of Arcadia
    Are most pleasing and give him joy.

Now the season brings thirst, yes, my Vergilius;[3]
But if you long to quaff vintage at Cales pressed,
You the favorite one, client of noble youths,
    You shall pay for your wine with nard.

Just a small onyx box full of a fragrant oil
Shall elicit a cask, which in Sulpician vaults[4]
Now lies—strong to give hope, new hopes and wash away
    All the bitterness of our cares.

If you haste to these joys, then with your wares come quick;
Since I do not intend for you to soak yourself
In my cups with no charge—just as though I were rich
    And at home in a house of wealth.

So have done with delays and with your zeal for gain;
And rememb'ring the black funeral fires while still
You may, mingle some brief folly with wisdom now:
  To be foolish is sweet at times.[5]

[1] Itys was the son of Tereus, a king of Thrace, and Procne, a princess of Athens. Tereus pretended that Procne was dead, and betrayed her sister Philomela. When Procne heard of this, she and her sister killed Itys and served him up at Tereus' table. Procne and Philomela then fled and only escaped from Tereus' vengeance by transformation into birds; Procne into a nightingale, and Philomela into a swallow, or vice versa as another form of the myth has it. Tereus himself was changed into a hoopoe. Horace apparently adopts the second form of the legend and means that the bird which mourns for Itys is the swallow.

[2] Attic: Procne and Philomela were the daughters of Pandion, the third mythical king of Athens.

[3] This can hardly be Vergil, the poet, for the phrases "client of noble youths" and "your zeal for gain" do not seem to apply; furthermore, Vergil, the poet, had been dead for six years when this book was published. The conjecture among scholars is that the reference is to a merchant, a doctor, or a dealer in unguents and perfumes. A physician dispensed his own drugs and would charge well for his precious nard.

[4] The Sulpician vaults, or storehouses, were probably located at the foot of the Aventine Hill in Rome.

[5] Metre: Third Asclepiadean.

They have heard, Lyce,[1] heard: my prayers the gods have heard:
They have heard, Lyce, heard: you are becoming old,
    Yet you wish to seem fair still,
        And you sport without shame, and drink,

And with quavering voice, drunken, you try to rouse
Sluggish Cupid. In the beautiful cheeks of fresh
    Chia he keeps his watch, her
        Skilled to play on the lute and sing.

For, disdainful, he flies quickly past withered oak,
And he flees from you now, shuns you, for blackened teeth
    And the snows of your head, yes
        And your wrinkles disfigure you.

Neither gauzes[2] of rich purple from Cos bring back,
Nor the costliest gems, days which swift-flying time
    Once for all in our annals
        Has recorded for all to read.

Whither fled is your charm; whither, alas, your bloom?
Where, the movements of grace? What do you have of her,
    Of her who breathed forth longing,
        Who had stolen me from myself?

And her face so divine, next after Cinara,
Winning, known for its wiles? Save that to Cinara
    The Fates gave but a few years;
        Lyce they meant to match in years

To the times of an old crow, so that ardent youths
Not without a good laugh, many a laugh, might look
    On a torch now burned down,
        Which has crumbled to scattered ash.[3]

---

[1] The old age of the wanton. Lyce is perhaps the same as in III, 10, though line 21 is against it.

[2] A costly gauzy silk much used by the demimonde and often mentioned by the Roman poets.

[3] Metre: Fourth Asclepiadean.

What zeal of Senate or the Quirítes[1] can
By full awards of honors, Augustus, thus
    Immortalize your virtues by their
        Graven inscriptions and public records,

O you who are, wherever the sun lights shores
Where living men dwell, greatest of princes? Who
    You are and what your might in warfare
        Have the Vindelici[2] learned—till now free

Of Latin mandates. For by your soldiery,
Intrepid Drusus drove out that ruthless race,
    The fierce Genauni,[3] overthrew the
        Fleet-footed Brenni[4] with heavy interest,

And strongholds set on terrible Alpine peaks;
The elder Nero[5] lately in heavy fight
    With signs and auspices propitious
        Routed completely the monstrous Rhaetians.

In martial combat splendid to watch was he;
With what disasters would he fatigue those hearts
    Resolved to die the death of freemen,
        Much as when Auster[6] the untamed billows

Keeps vexing when the band of the Pleiades
Tears clouds apart—as tireless was he to plague
    The foeman's troops and urge his raging
        Steed through the midst of the flames of battle.

As rolls the Aufidus[7] with his bull-like shape,
Which past Apulian Daunus's kingdom flows
    When he grows furious and plans some
        Terrible flood for the well-tilled lowlands,

So Claudius[8] with mighty attack o'erthrew
The iron-mail–clad ranks of the foreigners,
    And, mowing down the first and last lines,
        Victor without loss, he strewed the region,

With you supplying forces and strategy,
And your own gods. For when Alexandria,
    A suppliant, to you that day first
        Opened her port and her empty palace,

Propitious Fortune, three lustrums after that,
Did grant a favored end to hostility,
    And then to your campaigns completed
        Added the praise and the honor longed for.

To you the Indian, Mede, and Cantabrian[9]
Untamed before, the wandering Scythian,[10]
    All look with awe, O present guard of
        Italy and of great Rome, our mistress.

To you the Nile, who covers his secret springs,
The Ister,[11] and the Tigris which rushes on,
    The monster-teeming Ocean, that which
        Roars 'round far Britain, all yield obedience.

The land of Gaul that quakes not at death heeds you,
And that of stern Iberia lends its ears;
　　Sygambrians who joy in slaughter,
　　　　Arms laid to rest, now to you do homage.[12]

[1] A poetic variation of the official formula, *Senatus populusque Romanus*, the Senate and the Roman people. This is another ode in honor of Augustus and his two stepsons, Drusus and Tiberius.

[2] A Germanic people, whose chief town was Augusta Vindelicorum (the modern Augsburg.)

[3] A Germanic people, one of the tribes of the Rhaetians. They lived in the valley of the Inn.

[4] A Rhaetian tribe, living in the mountains north of the river Po. The name survives in the Brenner Pass.

[5] Tiberius, afterward emperor (14–37 A.D.).

[6] The dry, hot, south wind.

[7] A river of Apulia, swift and violent.

[8] Tiberius.

[9] The Cantabrians were a tribe of northwestern Spain.

[10] A nomadic tribe of northern Europe and Asia beyond the Black Sea.

[11] The lower part of the Danube river.

[12] Metre: Alcaic Strophe.

Phoebus rebuked me wishing to tell of war
And conquered cities, warning me with his lyre,
    Lest I should spread my puny sails o'er
        Waves of the Tuscan Sea. Your age, Caesar,[1]

Has brought to fields their plentiful fruits again,
Abundant crops, and once more to our own Jove
    Restored those standards[2] torn from haughty
        Parthian portals; and, freed from warfare,

Has closed the Gate of Janus Quirinus,[3] placed
A curb on license swerving beyond the path
    Of right, removed our faults, and called back
        Ways that we once knew, the old-time virtues,

Through which the Latin name and Italian strength
Have grown, the fame and majesty of our realm
    Have been extended from the Western
        Couch of the sun to his place of rising.

While Caesar is the guardian of our powers,
Not civil strife nor outrage shall drive away
    Our peace, nor wrath which forges swords and
        Sets wretched cities to strife and quarreling.

For neither those who drink of the Danube deep
Shall break the Julian edicts,[4] nor Getans, nor
    The Seres, nor the faithless Persians,
        Neither those born near the river Tanais.

And we, on both our working and festal days,
Amid the gifts of Liber, the jocund god,
   Our wives and children with us, duly
      First to the gods having prayed for blessing,

Accompanied by the Lydian flute, shall sing,
As was our fathers' wont, of those leaders done
   With valor, sing of Troy, Anchises,[5]
      And of the offspring[6] of kindly Venus.[7]

[1] The fourth book ends with a final tribute to Augustus and the empire.

[2] The Roman standards, which had been lost to the Parthians by Crassus at Carrhae, were recovered in 20 B.C. by Augustus' diplomacy. The Parthians were a Scythian people, famed in antiquity as roving warriors and skillful archers.

[3] The gateway of Quirinus, the Sabine war-god identified with Mars. The gates of the covered arcade passage in the Forum, commonly called the temple of Janus, were closed only in time of peace by the institution of Numa. They were shut once in the reign of Numa, once at the end of the First Punic War, and three times by Augustus.

[4] The ordinances of Augustus; not to be taken technically, though it suggests the Julian laws.

[5] The father of Aeneas, who bore him on his shoulders from the flames of Troy.

[6] Aeneas, the son of Venus and Anchises, and ancestor of the Romans.

[7] Metre: Alcaic Strophe.

"Exegi monumentum aere perennius."

APPENDIX

The Horatian Metres

THERE IS A FUNDAMENTAL DIFFERENCE in the construction of Latin poetry, which is quantitative, from that of English poetry, which is accentual. This is a result of the difference in character of the two languages. English is a strongly accented language, and English poetical form consists essentially of a certain succession of accented and unaccented syllables. Latin, on the other hand, is a quantitative language, and the rhythmic flow of Latin poetry was based, not upon accent, but upon a certain succession of long and short syllables, that is, upon the long and short intervals of time required for their pronunciation.

While accent in Latin was relatively subordinate, nevertheless in the reading of poetry the long syllables of fundamental feet received a certain prominence called "ictus," that is "blow" or "stroke." Since this ictus was not accent—neither stress accent nor musical accent—even the most careful translator would not reproduce precisely the effect of the ancient Latin metres unless he also employed syllables corresponding in length to those of the original; and, due to the difference in the construction of the two languages, this is practically impossible except perhaps for an occasional short passage. It is possible, however, to imitate very closely the musical

213

effect of the original metre by substituting the English accent for the Latin ictus; and this is the method followed in these translations.

From certain of the Greek lyric poets Horace borrowed thirteen metrical systems which he adapted to the Latin tongue and used with exquisite precision in writing the Odes. Since I believe that nothing is to be gained by confusing the casual reader by explanations of trochaic dipodies, cyclic dactyls, irrational long syllables, and other technical points of the metrical schemes, I have endeavored to reproduce here in greatly simplified form an approximation of each of these metrical systems by use of the diagrams commonly employed for English verse. The short horizontal lines indicate accented syllables, the curved lines the unaccented syllables; poetic feet are divided by single short vertical lines. Two short vertical lines mark the caesura, or natural rhythmic pause in the poetic line.

Identification

Alcaeus, a Greek poet of Lesbos, died about 580 B.C. He was a literary associate of Sappho. The Alcaic Strophe consists of four lines, the first three of which contain an extra-rhythmical upward beat (anacrusis) at the beginning of the line. This extra beat may be either a long or short syllable, and is indicated in the diagram below by the alternative symbols before the colon.

$$\gtrless : \ - \cup \ / - \cup \ / - \cup\cup \ / - \cup \ / -$$
$$\gtrless : \ - \cup \ / - \cup \ / - \cup\cup \ / - \cup \ / -$$
$$\gtrless : \ - \cup \ / - \cup \ / - \cup \ / - \cup$$
$$- \cup\cup \ / - \cup\cup \ / - \cup \ / - \cup$$

Alcman, a Greek poet of Sparta, flourished before 600 B.C. He was the founder of the Dorian school of choral lyric poetry. His verse was simple, clear, and musical, and was often sung at festivals and public functions. The Alcmanian Strophe consists of two lines, generally dactylic in character, though in some cases a second long syllable was used in place of two short ones.

$$- \cup\cup / - \cup\cup / - // \cup\cup / - \cup\cup / - \cup\cup / - -$$
$$- \cup\cup / - \cup\cup / - \cup\cup / - \cup$$

Archilochus, a Greek poet, was born at Paros about 700 or 650 B.C. His masterful iambic satire and his innovations in the use and construction of the personal lyric were admired by the ancients, and his style was imitated by other poets. Horace uses in the Odes only the First and Fourth of the Archilochian metres.

First Archilochian:

$$\cdot - \cup\cup / - \cup\cup / - // - \cup\cup / - \cup\cup / - \cup$$
$$- \cup\cup / - \cup\cup / \overset{\vee}{\underset{\wedge}{-}}$$

Fourth Archilochian:

$$- \cup\cup / - \cup\cup / - \cup\cup / - \cup\cup // - \cup / - \cup / - / -$$
$$\underset{\displaystyle\geq}{} : - \cup / - \cup / - \cup / - \cup / - / -$$

Asclepiades was a Greek poet of Samos, who flourished about 280 B.C. Five metrical schemes devised by him, and used later by Horace, may be described as follows:

First Asclepiadean:

$$- \cup / - \cup\cup / - // - \cup\cup / - \cup / -$$

Second Asclepiadean:

$$- \cup / - \cup\cup / - \cup / -$$
$$- \cup / - \cup\cup / - // - \cup\cup / - \cup / \overset{\vee}{-} \cdot$$

Third Asclepiadean:

$$- \, \cup \, / - \cup \cup / \stackrel{\llcorner}{} // - \cup \cup / - \cup / \stackrel{\vee}{=}$$
$$- \, \cup \, / - \cup \cup / \stackrel{\llcorner}{} // - \cup \cup / - \cup / \stackrel{\vee}{=}$$
$$- \, \cup \, / - \cup \cup / \stackrel{\llcorner}{} // - \cup \cup / - \cup / \stackrel{\vee}{=}$$
$$- \, \cup \, / - \cup \cup / - \cup / -$$

Fourth Asclepiadean:

$$- \, \cup \, / - \cup \cup / \stackrel{\llcorner}{} // - \cup \cup / - \cup / -$$
$$- \, \cup \, / - \cup \cup / \stackrel{\llcorner}{} // - \cup \cup / - \cup / -$$
$$- \, \cup \, / - \cup \cup / \stackrel{\llcorner}{} / -$$
$$- \, \cup \, / - \cup \cup / - \cup / -$$

Fifth Asclepiadean:

$$- \, \cup \, / - \cup \cup / \stackrel{\llcorner}{} // - \cup \cup / \stackrel{\llcorner}{} // - \cup \cup / - \cup / -$$

Sappho was the greatest of the early Greek lyric poets. She was born at Mytilene on the island of Lesbos during the early part of the sixth century B.C. She wrote in Aeolic dialect in a great many metres, one of which has been called after her, the Sapphic. Horace used this in twenty-six of his Odes, and the so-called Greater Sapphic in one more. They are indicated as follows:

Sapphic:

$$- \, \cup \, / - \cup \, / - \cup \cup / - \cup / - \cup$$
$$- \, \cup \, / - \cup \, / - \cup \cup / - \cup / - \cup$$
$$- \, \cup \, / - \cup \, / - \cup \cup / - \cup / - \cup$$
$$- \cup \cup / - \cup$$

Greater Sapphic:

$$- \cup \cup / - \cup / \stackrel{\smile}{} / -$$
$$- \cup / - \cup / - \cup \cup / \stackrel{\smile}{} // - \cup \cup / - \cup / \stackrel{\smile}{} / -$$

Sappho influenced many later poets, including Catullus, Ovid, and Swinburne, as well as Horace.

Horace also used in one ode (II, 18) a Trochaic Strophe, as follows:

$$- \cup - \cup / - \cup -$$
$$\stackrel{\smile}{} : \; - \cup - \cup // - \cup - \cup / \stackrel{\smile}{} \cup$$

In one Ode (III, 12) he used what is usually referred to as the Lesser Ionic, which is variously arranged by editors and metrists. The metrical scheme consists of ten pure Ionics, the fundamental foot being as follows:

$$\cup \cup - -$$

Horace's Odes should be read aloud; and, with a little practice and an occasional glance at the metrical scheme, the reader will be able to do this with comparative ease and added enjoyment, for only by an appreciation of the metrical flow of the poetry will the fullest understanding be obtained of its beauty. Then we can understand why, after two thousand years, the Odes of Horace are still a marvel and a delight.

GLOSSARY

Acheron—a river in the lower world.

Achilles—a Greek hero in the Trojan War.

Acroceraunium—a rocky promontory at the entrance to the Gulf of Oricum.

Aeneas—son of Venus and Anchises, hero of the Trojan War, and an ancestor of the Romans.

Aeolus—god of the winds.

Agrippa—M. Vipsanius, son-in-law of the Emperor Augustus and his right hand in war.

Alcaeus—lyric poet of Mytilene; inventor of Alcaic verse.

Anio—a river near Rome noted for its beauty.

Apollo—god of the sun, poetry, music, healing.

Apulia—a province of southeast Italy.

Aquilo—the north wind.

Archytas—a Pythagorean philosopher and mathematician, friend of Plato.

Athena—Pallas Athena, Greek goddess of war and wisdom.

Attalus—wealthy king of Pergamus.

Aufidus—a river of Apulia, swift and violent (now the Ofanto).

Augustus Caesar—first emperor of Rome.

Bacchus—god of wine and poets.

Bandusia—a pleasant fountain near Venusia, the birthplace of Horace.

Bassareus—a title of Bacchus.

Bellerophon—rider of the flying horse Pegasus, and slayer of the Chimaera.

Berecynthia—the goddess Cybele.

Caecuban—a fine wine.

Calends (Kalends)—the first day of the Roman month.

Campus Martius—a grassy plain in Rome along the river Tiber, and dedicated to Mars; used for games and recreation.

Cecrops—founder of Athens, the home of tragedy.

Cerberus—the three-headed dog of Pluto that guarded the entrance to the lower world.

Charon—the ferryman of the river Styx in the lower world.

Charybdis—a dangerous whirlpool between Italy and Sicily.

Chimaera—a fabulous monster (lion, goat, and dragon) slain by Bellerophon.

Chios—an island in the Aegean Sea.

Chloe—a woman's name.

Cinara—a woman friend of Horace.

Clio—the Muse of history.

Cocytus—a mythic river of the lower world.

Codrus—an early Athenian king.

Colchian—an inhabitant of Colchis, a province of Asia east of the Black Sea.

Corybantes—priests of Cybele.

Cyclades—islands in the Aegean Sea lying in a circle around Delos.

Cyclops—a race of giants with one eye in the middle of their foreheads.

Cynthia—the goddess Diana.

Cythera—an island in the Aegean Sea celebrated for the worship of Venus.

Daedalus—an Athenian who made wax wings for himself and his son Icarus.

Damalis—a woman's name.

Danaüs—a descendant of Inachus. He had fifty daughters.

Daunus—mythical king of Apulia.

Deiphobus—son of Priam, king of Troy.

Delos—an island in the Aegean Sea, birthplace of Apollo.

Delphi—city famed for its oracle of Apollo.

Diana—virgin goddess of the moon and of hunting; sister of Apollo.

Diespiter—the god Jupiter.

Dindymene—a goddess.

Diomedes—famous Greek hero at the siege of Troy.

Don—(ancient Tanais) a river in Russia.

Evius—a surname of Bacchus.

Falernus—an Italian region famed for its wines.

Faunus—god of agriculture and shepherds; later identified with Pan.

Favonius—the west wind.

Gades—a colony in Hispania, now the Spanish city of Cadiz.

Geloni—a Scythian people on the Borysthenes in modern Ukraine.

Genauni—a Germanic people in Rhaetia.

Getans—a Thracian tribe on the Danube River.

Glycera—a woman's name.

Grosphus—a Roman surname.

Hadria (Adria)—the Adriatic Sea.

Haemus—a mountain range in Thrace.

Hannibal—leader of the Carthaginians in the Second Punic War.

Hebrus—a beautiful youth; also a river in Thrace.

Hector—eldest son of Priam, king of Troy.

Helen—daughter of Jupiter and Leda, and wife of Menelaus. On account of her beauty, Paris carried her to Troy, and she thus became the cause of the Trojan War.

Helicon—a mountain of Boeotia, sacred to Apollo and the Muses.

Hercules—the god of strength.

Hyades—the "rain stars."

Hydaspes—a river in India.

Hylaeus—a centaur who offered violence to Atalanta.

Iapyx—the west-northwest wind.

Iberia—the Greek name of Spain.

Icaria—an island in the Aegean Sea.

Ida—a high mountain in Crete; also a high mountain in Phrygia near Troy.

Idomeneus—king of Crete, leader of the Cretans against Troy.

Ilium—Troy.

Inachus—first king of Argos, a Greek city.

Janus Quirinus—the Sabine god of war identified with Mars.

Jove (or Jupiter)—father of the gods.

Jugurtha—king of Numidia; conquered by Marius in the war with the Romans.

Lalage—a girl's name.

Lapithae—a people of the Thessalian mountain districts.

Latium—the country in Italy where Rome was situated.

Lesbos—an island in the Aegean Sea, home of the poet Sappho.

Lethe—the river of sleep and forgetfulness in the lower world.

Leuconoe—a man's name.

Liber—an old Italian god of fructification and planting, sometimes identified with Bacchus.

Libra—a southern zodiacal constellation.

Ligurinus—a man friend of Horace.

Lipara—an island near Sicily.

Liris—a river in Italy.

Lyce—a woman's name.

Lycidas—a beautiful young man.

Lyde—a woman's name.

Lydia—a woman's name; a friend of Horace.

Lustrum—a period of five years.

Maecenas—prime minister of Augustus, and patron of Horace the poet.

Mars—Roman god of war.

Martian Field—the Campus Martius (*q.v.*)

Medus—river in Persia.

Melpomene—the Muse of poetry.

Mercury—the messenger of the gods; the god of eloquence, gain, traders, and thieves.

Meriones—the charioteer of Idomeneus.

Minos—a judge in the lower world.

Mycenae—a city in Greece.

Neobule—a girl's name.

Nereus—a sea god.

Nones—the fifth day of every Roman month except March, May, July, and October, when it was the seventh.

Numantia—a city in Spain.

Olympus—a mountain in Thessaly, regarded as the seat of the gods.

Orcus—the lower world, the abode of the dead.

Parthians—a Scythian people, roving warriors and skillful archers.

Pegasus—the winged horse of the Muses.

Pelignian—pertaining to the territory of the Peligni in central Italy.

Pelops—son of Tantalus, king of Phrygia, father of Atreus and Thy-estes, grandfather of Agamemnon and Menelaus.

Phoebus—Apollo, god of the sun, poetry, music, and medicine.

Phyllis—a friend of Horace.

Pieria—a district of Macedonia; a district of Syria.

Pierides—the Muses.

Pindar—celebrated poet of ancient Thebes, a contemporary of Aeschylus.

Pindus—a lofty mountain in Thessaly.

Pluto—god of the lower world.

Pollux—and Castor; the constellation the Twins, the guide of mariners.

Prometheus—son of Iapetus and Clymene. He formed men from clay and animated them with fire stolen from heaven.

Proserpina—queen of the lower world, wife of Pluto.

Punic—relating to the ancient city of Carthage.

Pyrrha—a woman's name.

Quirinus—the name of Romulus after his deification.

Quirites—an ancient Sabine people; later Roman citizens.

Rhaetians—a mountain people north of the river Po.

Robigo—blight; worshipped as a deity to be propitiated.

Romulus—founder and first king of Rome.

Sabines—an ancient Italian people adjoining the Latins, and later united with them.

Salamis—an island in the Saronic Gulf; also a city on the island of Cyprus.

Sappho—ancient poetess of the Isle of Lesbos.

Scythians—a nomadic tribe of northern Europe and Asia beyond the Black Sea.

Semele—daughter of Cadmus and mother of Bacchus by Jupiter.

Seres—a people of eastern Asia (the modern Chinese).

Silvanus—a god of the woods.

Soracte—a mountain in Italy.

Sybaris—fictitious name of a young man.

Sygambrians—a powerful people of Germany.

Syrtis—a sand bank in the sea north of Africa.

Tartarus—the lower world.

Telegonus—son of Ulysses and Circe, who killed his father without knowing him.

Telephus—man's name; a friend of Horace.

Teucer—first king of Troy.

Thaliarche—master of the revels; a name coined by Horace.

Thetis—a sea-nymph.

Thrace—ancient country of southeastern Europe on the Aegean Sea.

Thyestes—brother of Atreus, who set before him for food the flesh of his own son.

Tiber—river in Italy.

Troy—city in northwest Asia Minor.

Tuscans—the inhabitants of Etruria in Italy.

Tyndaris—a woman friend of Horace.

Ulysses—king of Ithaca, leader of the Greeks in the Trojan War.

Varius—a Roman poet, friend of Horace and Vergil.

Varus—a Roman name.

Vesper—the evening star.

Vindelici—a Germanic people.

Voltur—a mountain in Apulia, southwest Italy.

Vulcan—the fire god.

GUIDE TO PRONUNCIATION

Achae'menēs

A'cheron, -'tia

Achil'lēs

Ācri'sius

Ācrocerau'nia

Ae'acus

Ae'fula

Aegē'an Sea

Ae'lius

Aenē'as

Aeo'lia

Ae'olus

Agamem'non

Agyi'eūs

Al'bius

Albun'ea

Alcae'us

Al'gidus

Alyat'tes

Amphī'on

Anac'reon

Anchī'ses

Androm'eda

An'i o

Antī'ochus

An'tium

Apū'lia

Archȳ'tas

Ariad'ne

At'talus

Ā'treūs

Au'fidus

Au'lon

Bā'iae

Ban'tia

Bārī'na

Bassa'reūs

Beller'ophon

Berecyn'thian

Bib'ulus

Bithyn'ia, -n

Bos'phorus

Brīsē'is

225

Cae'cuban
Calā'bria, -n
Ca'la is
Can'taber, -'brian
Cau'casus
Censorī'nus
Cer'berus
Charyb'dis
Chimae'ra
Chlō'e
Chlō'ris
Ci'nara
Cōcȳ'tus
Col'chis, -'chian
Coryban'tes
Corvī'nus
Co'tiso
Cȳ'cla dēs

Dā'cian
Daed'alus, Daedā'lian
Dam'alis
Dan'a ē, -'a id, -'a us
Dē iph'obus
Di es'piter
Dindymē'ne
Diomē'des
Dircāē'an

E'chion
Encel'adus
Enī'peūs
Eryman'thus
Ē'viad

Ē'vius

Fabri'cius
Faler'nus
Foren'tum

Gā'des
Galae'sus
Galatē'a
Genau'ni
Gē'ryon
Gly'cera
Gy'as
Gȳ'ges

Hae'mus
Has'drubal
Hel'icon
Hespē'rian
Hippol'yta
Hȳ'ades
Hydas'pes
Hȳlae'us
Hymet'tus, -'tian
Hyperborē'an

Īa'petus
Īa'pyx
Ī'bycus
Ic'cius
Īdae'an
Īdom'eneūs
Il'ium
Il lyr'ian

In'achus

Isth'mian

I'tys

Ixī'on

Lacō'nian

Laestrygō'nian

La'lagē

Lā ō'medon

La'pithae, -thae'ans

Larī'sa

Latō'e

Lenāē'us

Leucō'no e

Licym'nia

Ligurī'nus

Lol'lius

Lūce'ria

Lūcret'ilis

Lycae'an

Ly'ce

Lȳ'de

Lycō'ris

Lycur'gus

Maecē'nas

Mae on'ian

Marī'ca

Matī'num

Megil'la

Melpom'enē

Mēri on'ēs

Metau'rus

Metul'lus

Monae'ses

Mūrē'na

Mycēn'ae

Myg'don

Myr'ta le

Mytilē'ne

Ne ae'ra

Ne ar'chus

Ne obū'lē

Nē'reūs

Nī'o be

Niphra'tes

Nī'reūs

Nu'mida

Ō'ricum

Orī'on

Or'nytus

Pa'corus

Palinū'rus

Panae'tius

Pan'tho us

Parrha'sius

Pa'tara

Peg'asus

Pē'leūs

Pēlig'nian

Pē'lion

Pēnel'o pe

Pen'theūs

Phā'eton

Phalan'thus

Phi'dylē
Philip'pī
Phō'cis
Pho'lo ē
Phrahā'tēs
Phthī'an
Pi er'ia, -n
Pi er'idēs
Pimplē'a
Piri'tho us
Plē'iades
Pompē'ius
Pompi'lius
Porphy'rion
Pos'tumus
Praenes'te
Prōculē'ius
Prō'cyon
Proe'tus
Promē'theûs
Prōser'pina

Quinti'lius
Quin'tius, Hirpī'nus
Quirī'nus, Jā'nus
Quirī'tēs

Rho'do pē
Rhoe'tus
Rōbī'go

Sabae'an
Sal'amis
Sallus'tius

Sco'pas
Se'melē
Septi'mius
Sē'rēs, Sēr'ican
Sīthōn'ian
Sōrac'te
Spar'tacus
Stēsi'chorus
Sthe'nelus
Sy'baris ·
Sygam'bri, -'brian

Tae'narus
Ta'na is
Tan'talus
Taren'tum
Tar'tarus
Tecmes'sa
Tē'i an
Tel'amon
Tēleg'onus
Tē'lephus
Tem'pē
Thaliar'chus
Thy'ad, -dēs
Thyes'tes
Tīridā'tēs
Tīthō'nus
Tit'yos
Tydī'des
Tynda're us
Tyn'daris
Typhō'eûs

Ustī′ca

Venā′frum

Venus′ia, -an

Vergi′lius

Vindel′i ci

Xan′thus

7

The Odes of Horace has been set on the Linotype in ten-point
Electra, a face created by the American W. A. Dwiggins. Although
classed with the "modern" faces because of its square and flat serifs,
Electra exhibits the timeless features of traditional old-style types
which make for pleasurable legibility—qualities of design and read-
ability which fittingly complement the Odes of Horace.

NORMAN

UNIVERSITY OF OKLAHOMA PRESS

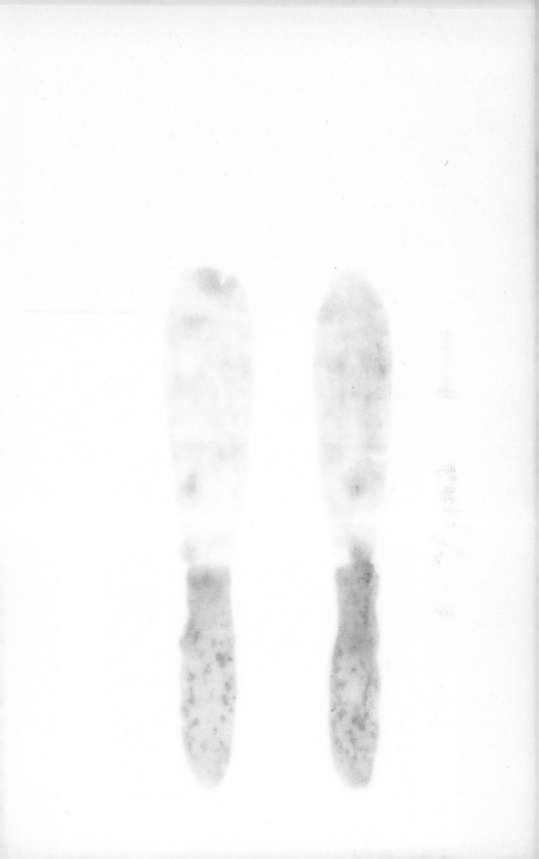

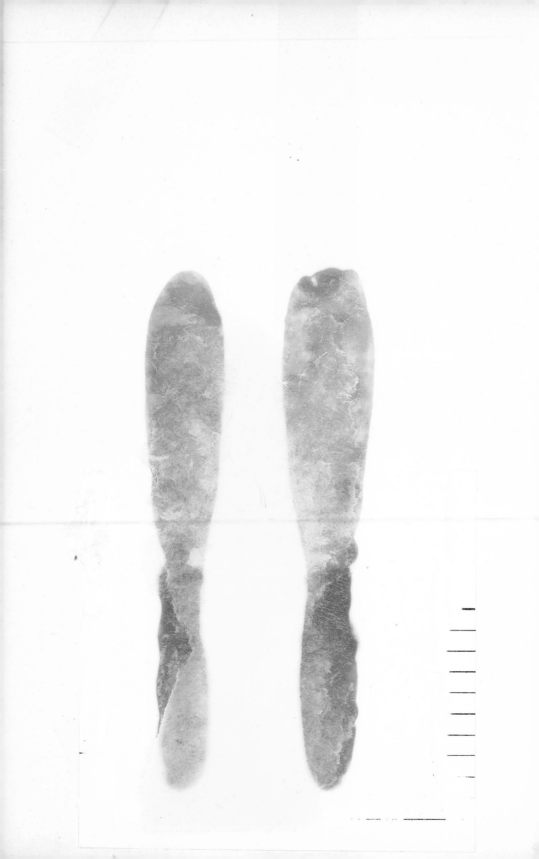